The School–Prison Trust

Forerunners: Ideas First

Short books of thought-in-process scholarship, where intense analysis, questioning, and speculation take the lead

FROM THE UNIVERSITY OF MINNESOTA PRESS

(Continued on page 130)

The School–Prison Trust

Sabina Vaught
Bryan McKinley Jones Brayboy
Jeremiah Chin

University of Minnesota Press
MINNEAPOLIS
LONDON

Excerpt from Tanaya Winder, "We Were Stolen," from *Why Storms Are Named After People and Bullets Remain Nameless,* CreateSpace Independent Publishing Platform, 2017; published by permission of the poet.

ISBN 978-1-5179-1426-4 (pb)
ISBN 978-1-4529-6804-9 (Ebook)
ISBN 978-1-4529-6836-0 (Manifold)

Published by the University of Minnesota Press, 2022
111 Third Avenue South, Suite 290
Minneapolis, MN 55401-2520
http://www.upress.umn.edu

Available as a Manifold edition at manifold.umn.edu

The University of Minnesota is an equal-opportunity educator and employer.

Dedicated to Jakes

Contents

Introduction: Conquest Projects

My crime is being an Indian. What's yours?

—LEONARD PELTIER, *Prison Writings: My Life Is My Sun Dance*

School: Coming for the Children

Far away from Leonard Peltier, Jacob sat in one state's prison for "juvenile offenders." He was seventeen, an enrolled member of his Tribal Nation, and had long since left high school on the Outside.

Jacob—Jakes, as the other incarcerated young men called him— laughed when I asked him about school one day.

We were sitting in the prison school's computer lab, which at that time was used only for a life skills class. Otherwise, it sat empty for hours, in dutiful observance of the no-internet policy for inmates. On that particular day, we grabbed a couple chairs at the small, round table that occupied the center of the room—a table from which life skills teachers could comfortably surveil the screens of all the computers, which were lined up along two long tables, leaning against two blank walls.

Jakes shifted uneasily in his cushioned chair. He looked down at the wood tabletop and circular coffee mug stains and adjusted his body repeatedly against the faded green office-weave fabric. These were provinces made foreign to him in the prison world of student chairs and tables, of plastic cell bunks, of total rules against crossing restricted territories of furniture.

"Weird, huh," I said.

"Yeah, man," and he looked down at either side of his lap, shifting again, until he looked up at me and took a nodding breath in. "OK."

We both laughed. Jakes was a tall, skinny kid. Approaching gangly, or perhaps departing from it as he moved toward uncertain adulthood. His face was a portrait of lovely contradictions. He looked out from deep-creased eyelids cradled in youthful, padded cheeks. The skin on his nose and forehead was unusually smooth, as unblemished as plain, light brown packaging paper, while acne scars corrugated his chin with the rugged mirage of stubble, and deepened the wells of his dimples, emphasizing his already winsome smile.

Sitting in that life skills room, we talked about video games, fishing, comics, and little brothers. It was a meandering conversation that at one point walked up to the front doors of Jakes' old school.

I asked him, "If maybe school was different on the Outside, do you think things would have turned out another way?"

"Shoot. Naw," he said. And he laughed hard—maybe at school, maybe at the futility of a question to which he thought I should or did know the answer. Maybe at the historicity of school as a coauthor of his *crime of being an Indian.*

The answer to the question of Jakes' alternate possible futures lies in the conquest colonial U.S. relation to young Native people, expressed in part in the history of U.S. Indian boarding schools.[1] School was the "last great Indian war."

"My grandfather Edward L. Hatchett was part of the government project to assimilate the Indians into the white man's society," writes Alan B. Walker. *"They concluded the only way to save the Indians was to destroy them and that the last great Indian war should be waged against children. They were coming for the children."*[2] Come for them they did. And come for them they continue.

We understand schools and prisons as a function of U.S. conquest statecraft—as part of a broad and deep war structure of *coming for children.* Conquest as a frame insists on observing colonial war as

1. Lomawaima and McCarty, "To Remain an Indian."
2. Walker, *Every Warrior,* 103, italics original.

the salient, ongoing shape and practice of state institutional and ideological worldmaking in what is called north america. In this book, we focus on the specifics of coming for *Native* children. This specificity deepens and complicates an analysis of school–prison relationships and, in so doing, opens up even more possibility—to revolt against common sense and its materialities, to identify common cause across peoples and ideas, and to consider urgent questions in relation to conquest capitalism (alongside others, we know all capitalism to be racial capitalism), Tribal Nation building, trusteeship, justice, sovereignty, self-determination, refusal, and freedom.

The Story of Jakes

This book is centrally the story of Jakes, Jakes' stories, and the stories they sparked in us. Jakes' practices of survivance and refusal—his Indigeneity, hilarity, brilliance, resistance—are instructive resurgent knowledge practices.[3] His stories are the heart of our dialectic journey. Jakes' stories are also ethnographic. We are no strangers to the irony of this fact. As Lakota scholar Vine Deloria Jr. writes, "into each life, it is said, rain must fall. . . . But Indians have been cursed above all other people in history. Indians have anthropologists."[4] While this book is not an ethnography of, about, or by Jakes, he ignited our thinking, and so we borrowed from ethnography's method and madness: it is contemporaneous, it is contextual, and it is relational.

Jakes' relationship with Sabina developed over the course of a long-term ethnographic project that took place largely in the prison school where he was incarcerated.[5] As relationships do, theirs con-

---

3. Simpson, *Always Done*; Vizenor, *Fugitive Poses*.
4. Deloria, *Custer Died*, 78.
5. Jakes was imprisoned at a facility where state-identified young men, ranging in age from fourteen to twenty-one and (with the exception of a few inmates) categorized by the state as Black, were sentenced to captivity. Part of the state captivity project—and part of the state Division of Juvenile Affairs' "treatment" across its locked facilities—was compulsory

tinued into ours and became part of the relationships that guided our writing. Jakes inspired us. Made us laugh. Found his way in our daily correspondences. It became clear to us that Jakes was not just a subject through whom we iterated ideas. We were inspired by him to be more imaginative. He felt at times like a family member and a coauthor, and even sometimes like our younger selves. We developed fervent wishes for him: a free future, meaning, a place. In short, a different world. In the face of a crushing system, Jakes was funny as hell. He resisted. He refused. But he was also sad, mean, boring, smart. He lived in all the equally profound and mundane ways one does. And this living grabbed us. It is a kernel of the thinking in the pages that follow. So Jakes' stories and dialogues shape this book. While he is a protagonist in our thinking, and while we grew to love and appreciate him even in his physical absence, we are careful not to over attribute ideas, intentions, and interpretations. We do not romanticize him as a sage, absent interlocutor but rather seek to honor him as present in our relationships and thinking.

Centering the intimate life of Jakes' will and relationality in a cluster of systems, we are disinterested in sham platitudes or trite proclamations and instead continually push the tendrils of our inquiry outward, tracing the outlines and rough edges of school–prison relations. In this regard, the pursuits of this book are simple: to attend deeply to Jakes' stories; in that attention, to invite readers to consider a constellation of legal, historical, and contemporary forces that drive and shape the school–prison relationship for some Native young people, families, communities, and Nations; and to take up these attentions and considerations through a lens of self-determination.

---

schooling. Vaught, *Compulsory*. Captivity and its instruments are removal projects that banish the captive person from relations to people and place, endeavoring to erase their interconnected existence even as their image may be magnificently distorted as a categorizing projection onto the stage of societal order: the criminal and the inmate.

A More Sophisticated Technique

"After the Revolution," writes Vine Deloria Jr.,

> the new United States adopted the doctrine of discovery and continued the process of land acquisition. The official white attitude toward Indian lands was that discovery gave the United States exclusive right to extinguish Indian title of occupancy either by purchase or conquest. It turned out that the United States acquired the land neither by purchase nor by conquest, but by a *more sophisticated technique* known as trusteeship.[6]

For Native peoples, trusteeship is a complex legal and political relationship, evolving most concretely from the colonial ideologies embedded in U.S. Supreme Court chief justice John Marshall's proclamation that Tribes are "domestic dependent nations" whose "relation to the United States resembles that of a ward to his guardian."[7] This delineation of subjected dependency codified an intractable paternalism of imposed federal Trust over Native sovereignty. The federal Trust "responsibility" grew from the conquest, colonial assertion that Tribal Nations could not completely self-govern—even if their sovereignty was inherent, their governance was and is dependent and subject to federal superintendence. This "responsibility," inaugurated through the coercive establishment and breaking of treaties that wrested land from peoples, is violently asymmetrical and in keeping with other U.S. conquest responsibilities. For instance, Truman claimed that the atomic bomb was a god-given "responsibility" to be used for "His purposes" by the United States. With Native Nations, the United States defines its "responsibility" as an absolute congressional authority to terminate, modify, or otherwise fulfill the Trust relationship, feeding a system of colonial paternalism that undermines Indigenous sovereignty.

6. Deloria, *Custer Died*, 31, italics added.
7. Cherokee Nation v. Georgia, 18.

In our consideration of this *more sophisticated technique* in the context of schools and prisons, we remain respectful of the ingenuity and imagination of Indigenous peoples in leveraging the Trust relationship for the benefit and survivance of Indigenous Nations. Our focus is on how trusteeship continuously reestablishes colonial conditions through schools and prisons.

Tracing one strand of a genealogy of conquest, carceral state trusteeship, in this book, we situate school as the axial apparatus of the massive Trust project aimed at the temporally and materially rehearsed dispossession of Native peoples' futures. More specifically, we consider the rise of what we propose as the *school–prison trust*— and its imaginary ameliorative practices of treatment, restoration, and justice in relation to Native young people across contexts—as linked to broader U.S. trends and as a distinctive function of ongoing trusteeship. The school–prison trust frames the unique legal and historical relationships among schools, prisons, the state, and Native communities and young people who shape the ongoing war against Native children.

Schools and Prisons

Our work draws from, is indebted to, and is in conversation with the extraordinary body of scholarship on school–prison relations in the United States. This work helps us consider the complex controlling relationships among schools, prisons, and other carceral apparatuses and institutions.

In particular, we are influenced by the work of two people. Erica Meiners brought sharp attention to the relationships between schools and prisons and also introduced the concept and practice of abolition to the field of education. Damien Sojoyner, whose framing of school–prison relations, enriched by his careful local attentions to the Southern California context and Black Los Angeles, upends absolutist notions of state power that infiltrate some of the work on what was originally called the school-to-prison pipeline. He argues for a relational dynamism that understands the structured repression of Black people in schools as the shifting expression of a complex history of power contestations, movements, and more. "The structure of public education is responding to the actions taken by Black students that are perceived to threaten the status quo," writes Sojoyner.

> In this regard, the criminalization of Black youth is not only intentional, but it is in response to direct agitation on the part of Black people. . . . The modes of current school discipline (e.g., policing and expulsions) have developed in an attempt to suppress assertions of Black culture, Black autonomy, and Black liberation movements within schools.[8]

This notion—that the repressive, controlling functions of carceral educational institutions are counterinsurgent responses to the will, resistance, and efforts of young people and their communities (and, we suggest, Indigenous culture, Indigenous autonomy, and Indigenous liberation movements, and as intertwined with Black)—governs the grammar of our dialogue into the school–prison trust. As we take notice of state and social structure, action, and contradiction, we are centered in Indigeneity. This does not diminish the unfathomable regularity and unbearably brutal nature of conquest violence; rather, it highlights the viability of sovereignty and self-determination.

For us, incorporating questions of trusteeship into the school–prison relationship conversation is about navigating a confluence of critical influences, through which we engage some contemporary carceral manifestations of conquest colonization as they pronounce cloudy legal technologies to dissemble unqualified state power. And it is about offering greater dimension to the collective understanding through reflections on Jakes' stories and their illumination of murky corners of our own knowledge. We are not

8. Sojoyner, "Black Radicals," 245.

setting out to assert a new and distinguishing frame or to rename the already existing.

As we journey with Jakes through the stories of his subjection to the school–prison trust, and as we mark those with our reflections on the tangle of conquest colonial statecraft, we hear in, with, and from Jakes the power of reclaimed times and freedom temporalities; the unbreakable joy of life-giving, hilarious, and resistive names; the eager balm of relationships and relationality; and the fearlessness of refusal and survivance.

But first we consider trusteeship.

War Genealogies

The origin stories of the school–prison trust have no explicit starting point or beginning, and as such we do not bind our conceptualization of this constellation of historical points to one single framing. We see relevant frames for understanding across many scholarly conversations and traditions, some of which are currently in generative tension with one another. And we find it essential to remain grounded in Black intellectual traditions that offer vigorous analyses of colonialism and conquest. Coming from different scholarly traditions, the three of us share a rejection of the odd and yet chronically reproduced bifurcation that Indigenous reads land and Black reads labor or that Indigenous reads "bodies" for genocide and settlement and Black reads "bodies" for slavery and death; the propertized notion that firstness privileges relationship to land and that diaspora unmoors from land; and the reduction of Black and Indigenous to proprietary and exclusive material, historical, cultural, phenotypic, and ontological categories. Our turns to law, state institutional practice, and warfare are in small part a generative rebuttal, not the least of which is to ourselves.

We begin by tracing the particular genealogy of the school–prison trust through three statecraft codification junctions we demarcate as discovery, property, and trusteeship. Later, we join these canonical, juridical histories with the material and cultural arcs of colonization that form the moontides of conquest colonialism: accumulation, labor, and production. Our intercession, then, is not only not chronological but also not subsequential. Among our intellectual guides, we take as a north star in our thinking Cedric Robinson's durable historical guide to racialization, capitalism, and colonization. That is, to start with, that colonialism, racialism, and imperialism were long-standing projects in europe prior to conquest outside that "continent" and that racial regimes born of european ideology are brutal but flimsy:

> Racial regimes are constructed social systems in which race is proposed as a justification for the relations of power. While necessarily articulated with accruals of power, the covering conceit of a racial regime is a makeshift patchwork masquerading as memory and the immutable. . . . But racial regimes are unrelentingly hostile to their exhibition. This antipathy exists because a discoverable history is incompatible with a racial regime and from the realization that, paradoxically, so are its social relations. . . . Employing mythic discourses, racial regimes are commonly masqueraded as natural orderings, inevitable creations of collective anxieties prompted by threatening encounters with difference. Yet they are actual contrivances, designed and delegated by interested cultural and social powers with the wherewithal sufficient to commission their imaginings, manufacture, and maintenance.[9]

As we go, we will consider some of the specific ways racial regimes' simultaneously evasive and bold invented memories, false encounters, and mythic origins masquerade as natural orderings through the well-commissioned school–prison trust. And we will consider how social relations and their histories upend this taken-for-granted system.

We take as yet another celestial body in the sextant of our thinking the understanding that the war of conquest is ongoing. In Vizenor's "Custer on the Slipstream," one character says to another,

> Everywhere else the government restores the nations they defeat in wars. Do you know why the Indian nations, the proudest people in the

9. Robinson, *Forgeries*, xii–xiii.

whole world, were never restored? . . . The answer is simple. . . . This is
the answer, listen now, because we were never defeated, never defeated, that is the answer. . . . We get nothing, nothing, because the white
man never defeated us, but he makes his living on us being poor.[10]

Perhaps defeat requires surrender, or withdrawal of the aggressing
armies, or the recognition of the parties involved—or some com-
bination of those. Whatever the markers and flags of defeat might
be, nowhere do they exist for Native Nations and people in what
is called the United States. The trails of massacre, terror, violence,
enslavement, slaughter, containment, subjugation, settlement, termination, removal, repression, and impoverishment are worn deep
on the earth. But none arrives at an end point. We understand these
as interrelated acts of supreme violence that can result in what
might be total annihilation of communities and peoples but do not
require and in fact override the relational conditions for surrender
and defeat.

The particular form of colonialism practiced in what is called the
U.S. today is yet unsettled. Conquest—a colonial form of warcraft—is
a salient feature of the dynamic power context we begin to wonder about in these pages. A colonial state is perpetual conquest—
warcraft and statecraft occupy the same institution. Without a
declared war in progress, and a litany of battles to mark it, the very
structure of colonial power remains war. Conquest does not require
overt "exploration" or "discovery" as catalysts or features (though
they often serve as valorized retrospective justifications that map
dominant european moral, epistemic stances). Conquest serves
itself. And such plunder has no confusingly virtuous, enlightened,
or innocent motives. Extraction, exploitation, and profit are acceler-
ants to war's inferno. Occupation is a tactic, and occupied territories
are an arena of war.

Although we draw also from settler colonialism—Audra Simpson's
work, for instance, is core to large portions of our inquiry—we are

10. Vizenor, "Custer," 21.

not trying to make a settler-colonial argument. Partly because we feel inadequate to the task and partly because conquest and war help us better understand the questions of the school–prison trust with which we struggle here. Much of the scholarship and policy around the Trust relationship center on governance and control over Native land and resources—property rights as defined in colonial law.[11] Trusteeship describes the state's mechanized understanding of its coercive, asymmetrical responsibility to all that it understands as Native property. This relationship is transactional and asymmetrical or unidirectional.

In this propertized schema, children have proven to be among the most valuable property. In describing part of the ongoing practice of trusteeship, Fletcher and Singel write, "Indian children . . . remain a primary focus of the federal government's duty of protection, now known as the federal general Trust relationship."[12]

Among many other things, American Indian[13] children are actual and symbolic purveyors of Indigenous knowledges, future protectors and potential beneficiaries of land and water, and titleholders to dual citizenship. Children are possibility. They may become co-operative, assimilated, disruptive, colonial, revolutionary. Docile, vanishing subject, nothing of note, or trouble. They may become necessary labor, or surplus labor, or inadequate labor. Or revolutionary labor. In some ways, Native children confound colonial properties and so threaten to upend ongoing carceral state projects of possession. What we call the school–prison trust is a decisive weapon in the arsenal of *the last great Indian war . . . waged against children.* Though we are describing here a particular war against Native children through law and policy, we understand these as part

11. Newton, "Enforcing."

12. Fletcher and Singel, "Indian Children," 964.

13. The designations and self-identifications of *American Indian, Indian, Native, Native American, Indigenous,* and more have meanings that shift with context, purpose, and peoples. We use terms to best align with context and people.

of a system of war that is necessary to establishing and maintaining the colonial state—an active war against children that includes the caging of children at the U.S. borders, assaults on young activists, denial of climate change, state violence, and numerous other manifestations of violence against the future.

And because, as Vizenor's character explains of ongoing war, "the white man never defeated us, but *he makes his living* on us being poor,"[14] we are interested not only in how conquest, with its profit motives, is in dialectic with the labor questions at the heart of carcerality[15] but also in how the refusal of surrender is a sustained, continuous, and mighty practice of self-determination against a racial capitalist order.

We understand the following schema of three statecraft codification junctions of discovery, property, and trusteeship as elaborated in the interacting, millennia-old, imperial contexts of conquest.

Discovery

One of many lineages of the school–prison trust can be found in the european codification of discovery through a fifteenth-century papal bull.[16] Papal bulls, declarations, or issuances were not uncommon and were frequently mercantile or political in nature and intent. These were holy imprints of the fascist formulations by which the Roman Catholic Church cemented capitalist class relations to the existence of nation-states and sanctified those relations through demonic global dominion over land through human possession and dispossession. Ensuing nation-state legal iterations are in palimpsest relation to these covenant bulls. Bull *Inter Caetera* made discovery doctrinal through key features: making inhabitant coterminous with Christian, such that lands inhabited by non-Christian peoples

14. Vizenor, "Custer," 21.
15. Rodriguez, *Forced Passages*; James, *Warfare*; Davis, *Are Prisons Obsolete?*; Gilmore, *Golden Gulag*; Sojoyner, *First Strike*.
16. Newcomb, *Pagans*.

were thereby uninhabited and discoverable; establishing discovery as a political-economic relationship among conqueror nations mediated by the Church.[17] It also deepened the ways "discovery" and "exploration" were embedded across broad sectors of european epistemic life, from science (where they are still confused with "curiosity" and valorized through so-called universally beneficial solutions) to art (where the pursuit of individual expression can promote imperialism with impunity).

Discovery is a matter-of-fact precondition for sanctified exploitation and accumulation; an ideology of relations that marches conquest forward in myriad ways; and a conceptual, historical, legal inception point and ongoing ideological device for the school–prison trust. Discovery is both a powerful implement and a weapon of a vulnerable regime.

Discovery iteratively sanctifies the myth of vacancy—of land, resources, people, knowledge—as sustained, solemn truth. In this way, ideological power resides not in the initial conquest claim of vacancy or even in the consecrated rationales for warfare and removal of peoples from lands (although those are deathly necessary to maintaining the myth) but rather in the incessant reenactment and rearticulation of discovery across scale as a feature intrinsic to conquest life. This barbarous dissemblance confesses the feeble infrastructure of conquest and its habituated desperation—discovery is both a real experience and a fictive device of conquest by which the colonial state announces its importance and reassures those in power that the destruction of others is warranted.

Conquest thrives on what Felix Cohen termed "transcendental nonsense"—laws' manipulative, "trapezing" reliance on narrow, precedent language to iteratively stamp absurd (and violent) judgments with rational legitimacy.[18] Discovery—as a stance and act of

---

17. Miller, "Doctrine of Discovery."
18. Cohen, "Transcendental Nonsense," 814.

conquest war—trapezes as such. Discovery unfolds across multiple planes, tautologically transmuting into commonsense.

Discovery in relation to Native Nations and the United States finds particular legal expression through tautological commonsense in the first two cases of the Marshall Trilogy. The Supreme Court outlines white rights of possession and dominion of the United States over Native lands and peoples through european law prior to the formation of the early republic.[19] In *Johnson v. M'Intosh,* the Court firmly entrenched the "doctrine of discovery" by finding in favor of M'Intosh, who bought the land in question from the United States. Johnson, on the other hand, was one of many land speculators who bought the land directly from the Piankeshaw, not from the British government ("the Crown"), before the United States asserted nationhood and before the Trade and Intercourse Acts of 1795 prohibited such a sale outright.

Chief Justice John Marshall's opinion in *Johnson* reified this hierarchy of discovery in ownership, identifying Indigenous peoples as "the conquered": occupants—first *on* the land, but never possessors *of* the land. He writes,

> The United States . . . maintain, as all others have maintained, that discovery gave an exclusive right to *extinguish the Indian title of occupancy, either by purchase or by conquest.* . . . The title by conquest is acquired and maintained by force. The conqueror prescribes its limits. Humanity, however, acting on public opinion, has established, as a general rule, that the conquered shall not be wantonly oppressed, and that their condition shall remain as eligible as is compatible with the objects of the conquest. . . . This opinion conforms precisely to the principle which has been supposed to be recognized by all European governments, from the first settlement of America. *The absolute ultimate title has been considered as acquired by discovery.*[20]

---

19. The third case in the Marshall Trilogy, Worcester v. Georgia, 31 U.S. 515 (1832), is important to Federal Indian Law in solidifying the exclusivity of the relationship between the federal government and Tribal governments, to the exclusion of state law.

20. Johnson v. M'Intosh, 588–89, 592, emphasis added.

In the discovery-driven logic of absolute conquest, land exchange was only valid between european, or european-derived, colonial governments, which would then grant a patent or property right to the land to a legal individual. Lands under Native guardianship could only be acquired by another government by treaty (between nations) or through warfare.

This Doctrine of Discovery is a cornerstone to the law of property and property rights in the United States—constructing a system of ownership cemented in overlapping, coproducing conquest systems of dispossession, possession, genocide, and carcerality. Discovery gives way to the totalization of individualized, righted, transactional ownership and the decimation of relationship with land. This counterfeit property is then always a profit of war, a plunder relying on white supremacy and property law to obfuscate and naturalize human rights violations: "a matter of imperial policy masquerading as historical fact."[21]

Moreover, this conquest plunder is invented in relation to extinguishable "Indian title," legitimating the maintenance of profit "by force" and ascribing Native people to the general subhuman category of the *conquered,* but also whose *condition shall remain as eligible as is compatible with the objects of the conquest,* which are at least capitalist and extractive—so, in other words, as discovered and ancillary objects of economy. Discovery demands domination as a principal feature of relationality. And it advances revisionist amnesia as an antidote to barbaric origins. Discovery is an announcement of white colonial divine right of power onto and over Indigeneity: lands, Nations, labor, knowledge, children, and futures. It continuously predicts an attempt either to claim the Indigenous as property or to hold what cannot be owned in a noncorrespondence relation of nation-to-nation Trust, to assert dominance and control indefinitely. The extinguishment of Indigenous rights is one threshold and condition of land ownership in the

21. Trask, *Native Daughter,* 31.

United States. Extinguishment of Indigenous rights inaugurates one production of property. But what exactly is property?

Property

A profit of conquest war, property in the United States is a system in the tradition of British common law, forged in the ruthless economic, political, and cultural landscapes of europe and (re)constructed through staggering exercises of power, such as slavery. From the very beginning of the new United States, humanity itself was codified via property; humanity was made through a ruthless and total merger of land control, maleness, whiteness, Protestantism, and more.[22] This codification of property and possession was directly descended from an inveterate european racial hierarchy that violently assembled whiteness, racialism, and racial capitalism through a long tradition of conquest, domination, and racial differentiation via caste and nationality. It began in europe, by europeans, on europeans.[23] This tradition became a form of consciousness.

In the new United States, rights became the form and the proxy for property; so, in that exclusive, narrow humanity was the cornerstone: not only the right to own people, land, and a host of material and immaterial goods—deeds, contracts, and on, ad infinitum—but also the twinned right to own one's self and never to be owned. Among many functions, these properties of the self embedded the custom and command of the Doctrine of Discovery— the right to ascertain something uninhabited and so to reasonably, accurately, or legally possess it. U.S. rights—prerequisite for and signaling legal humanity—then are organized through the possession–dispossession dyad and constitute american democracy through individual discovery. Conquering is the right to own one's self. This individual right to conquer is sanctified or denied in an endless, accumulative relationship between the citizen and

---

22. Harris, "Whiteness as Property," 1721–22.
23. Robinson, *Black Marxism*, 66.

the state. The citizen and the conqueror are fused. Because rights in the United States are largely celebrated, asserted, and desired as a moral good, conquest as sustained warfare and statecraft is more than just a central feature of the american state and its allied citizenries; conquest is the shape of U.S. democracy.

White state and citizen possession relies on the discovery and plunder of global Indigenous peoples—dispossession as a practical matter in the expropriation of land and resources, through discovery, and through extraction and accumulation of people to be shuttled into various extraction and accumulation projects.[24] Indigenous possessory interests were fabricated, then rendered imperfect, fraudulent, and irrelevant to discovery, claim, and possession. Unshackled by moral contradiction, conquest dispossession is the production of a convoluted vacancy: for the land to be discovered, it must first be vacant, but the Doctrine of Discovery (and the specific euro-epistemic conventions of humanity it advances) premises vacancy on Indigenous peoples being initially present on the land. The Christian land grab, the interminable drive to establish divine dominion over all life, does not respond to the problem of people present. Rather, as evidenced in U.S. law, discovery (and so conquest) requires and predicts peoples, then codifies the specificities of that presence through the productions of vacancy. In U.S. law, this vacancy is accomplished by the codification of rights that not only permit but definitionally require vacating peoples of possessory rights, which in turn consecrates the conquest project of peoples being vacated of life (through various conquest projects of genocide, removal, and so on). The land is rendered vacant as the peoples present are vacated of nonuniversal, exclusive, possessory rights required for humanity in conquest law. Vacancy absolves deliberate conquest from colonization and eases the way for an insidious enactment and expression of discovery as settlement of emptiness. This discoverable vacancy is a site of acute, perennial contestation against Native life.

24. Coulthard, *Red Skin*.

Central to our thinking about the school–prison trust is the merger of discovery and property, enacted in the dis/possession of humans. Because children are not actually imbued with the subject rights of citizens, they were and are more easily incorporated into the practice and logic of possession and its inherent dispossession. Linked to discovery-for-accumulation conquest labor and land logics, possession extended to nonwhite children through various slave codes, among others, played on the rare and exclusive rights of self-ownership. One cannot own children without owning one's self. Therefore, in examining the school–prison trust, we appraise some of the ways possessory rights are axial to carceral praxes and the U.S. colonial conquest dimensions of dispossession, nation building, and citizenship. In the various codifications of nonwhiteness as subhuman or conquest object-subject, nonwhite children were converted as property of both propertied whites and the state. Because property is a status, system, possession, and right as well as a mediator of rights, codification of children as property refers to all these and the subsequent treatment they allow and encourage. In the case of Native children, propertization categorizes them as uninhabited and discoverable and subjects determination of their lives to state superintendence. And, because Indigenous Knowledge Systems actively rebut property, Native children are an uninterrupted and robust threat to conquest.

Trust

Discovery and property merge in total, depraved fidelity in the legal construction of federal trusteeship over Tribal Nations. The Trust relationship is infected by a specific conquest paternalism illustrated in the second case of the Marshall Trilogy, *Cherokee Nation v. Georgia.* In his opinion, Chief Justice Marshall conceptualizes Indian Nations as "in a state of pupilage." Furthermore, he writes, "Their relation to the United States resembles that of a ward to his guardian."[25] Specifically, Deloria points out, Marshall "classified

25. *Cherokee Nation,* 17.

the Cherokees as a 'dependent domestic nation,' a definition that has plagued everyone ever since."[26] The particular plague took the shape of trusteeship—vesting control and ownership in the hands of the federal government and conditioning Native possession and sovereignty on federal superintendence.

Trusteeship relies on the creation of property through colonial domination, extinguishing Indigenous claims "by purchase or conquest"[27] to create possessory rights—and associated individual rights under the law—for certain white males to own, inherit, and bequeath.[28] Individual rights, domination, and possession are the foundational holy trinity of colonial law. This trinity played itself out through specific mechanisms determined against the peoples and contexts to be dominated and the colonial selves to be humanized.[29]

Chief Justice Marshall mechanized a diminished capacity for sovereignty through a federal legal obligation for structured paternalism and, we argue, maternalism. The relegation of entire Nations to a condition of pupilage maps the relationship between state and student and nation-state and Tribal Nation. Tribal Nations are subjected to a federal oversight that carries a moral imperative and legal authority for the regulation, detention, supervision, and reeducation of Native peoples—particularly young people. Strikingly, the guardian–ward relationship of trusteeship is limitless, as Congress holds "plenary power" to define or terminate the Trust responsibility. This responsibility may be used to enforce obligations to Tribal Nations guaranteed by treaty or stat-

26. Deloria, *Indian Declaration of Independence,* 115. Importantly, Deloria's writing inverts Marshall's declaration of "domestic dependent" to "dependent domestic." We are unsure of his intent but think it significant since the order of the words highlights the conditions imposed by the Court—dependence and domesticity are both relative, and subservient to the United States.

27. *Johnson,* 574.

28. Harris, "Whiteness as Property."

29. Deloria, *Custer Died*; Morrison, *Playing in the Dark*; Wynter, "Unsettling the Coloniality."

ute. The United States maintains a superintendence through Trust that centers Congress's power. Plenary power is power *without limit* or review. It is absolute.

Trust is, then, a form of war powers—active or indolent—that undergirds a carceral state. It is a more sophisticated war technique. And its signal technology is school. It is a war on children.

War Powers

The *sophisticated technique* of trusteeship is in part its inextricable embeddedness in federal law and policy: all attempts to end trusteeship are techniques to end federal recognition of sovereignty and self-determination, and so have been "uniformly disastrous" for the Tribal Nations subjected to the Termination era.[30] As trusteeship continues, young Native people are both assets and rightful "beneficiaries" of the trusteeship. And ancillary objects of its conquest market drives. This creates a paradoxical guarantee that trusteeship never ends: it is a paternalistic "protection" from harm yet is itself a conquest harm, one made necessary for its own continuation.

We explore what we term the school–prison trust to highlight the ways in which the web (of carceral state institutions, conquest colonial ideologies and their legal-material expressions, and racial capitalist structures) that ensnares young people into a perpetual system of exploitation, dispossession, and appropriation takes on particular meaning and shape for Native young people, communities, and Nations. Schools and prisons are two central and interrelated institutions through which trusteeship is exercised, even when the movement of young people across them is neither explicitly determined by Trust nor understood by state agents as a distinct process. Across these fastened institutions, Indigenous children are discovered—along the route to white accumulation and salvation—as not properly owned by Native family, mother,

30. Canby, *Nutshell,* 62.

community, or Nation. They are discovered as familially, culturally, and politically uninhabited and incapable of sovereign inhabitation. In other words, Native young people are predetermined as existing in a context of parental vacancy (the unit relevant to dominant legal ideology) and vacated parental rights.

If discovery is the attempt to possess what must be established as previously unknown, vacant, and without antecedent in western epistemology—but also peopled—then the axiological inauguration of the Native child and so Native schooling is palpable and un-staunched: *terra nullius* in humans accomplished through bodily, social, cultural, ecological, linguistic, and political unknowing of generationality. They are possessed by the school–prison trust, designated a priori as in need of removal, purchase, modification, and/or destruction. They are impossible possessions of a people ideologically and legally marked as incapable of full possession. They are useless capital accumulation and simultaneous threat to the existence of the U.S. empire. Hence the school–prison trust describes the network of discovery, property, and Trust ideological and material systems administered by endemic necessity on young Native people. It is a sophisticated war technique of brute force and frail dynasties.

In the specific context of the school–prison trust, we observe what diabolically charades "as moral humanitarian intervention" acting "without equal regard for . . . 'sovereignty.'"[31] Trusteeship, an ongoing war power of the Doctrine of Discovery and the codification of racial property, mobilizes a *more sophisticated technique* that makes what should be the extralegal removal of Indigenous children the legal removal into schools and prisons. Moreover, trusteeship—asymmetrical, paternalistic, and proprietary—is always about termination. It ensures contingent, tentative, and terminable sovereignty. Termination-driven trusteeship infuses the purposes and praxes of schooling and incarceration.

31. Million, *Therapeutic Nations*, 11.

And yet all this—discovery, property, Trust, termination, and the seemingly endless arsenal of conquest war—is a sloppy, brutal, and sustained cluster of ideologies, mechanisms, and practices precisely because conquest is cowardly. Conquerors and their agencies and governments, their private systems and capitalist cancers from not-for-profits to transnational corporations, undertake their destruction from a defensive stance. Defensiveness is the nature of greed. Greed is imbued with a raw, warped, unsettling knowledge that the means of dispossession might be available to others. Greed is a dragon living on a hoard of treasure, fashioning fortressed lairs of sedentary self-captivity and venturing out with erratic adrenaline, only to scorch the totality of life around its lair. Conquerors dedicate enormous resources to the bulwark of ideology to protect against the will, the life, and the power of those whose resources they want, whose docility they desire but cannot obtain, and whose existence calls into question their gods and their ghosts.

A Snowy Day

I wasn't paying too much attention to Jakes. Mostly because I was paying attention to myself and Ace. An hour or so earlier, I had sat in the waiting area at the entrance of the prison, witnessing Ace's mom be turned away by security staff. It was a snowy day, and she had taken off work, gotten a ride, and come up to the prison to drop off socks and other personal items Ace needed. She was told there was a new policy: because the young men were getting "contraband" during visits, she could not leave the items. (It made no sense and all the sense: capriciousness is a carceral logic.) She was told Ace didn't really need anything anyway. She told the staff, "Tell Ace I love him," and she left her mother-gifts on the counter and walked out the heavy metal door into the sodden snow.

In the classroom, I watched Ace, wondering how long I should wait, or should I wait, or what was I waiting to tell him. We know things about other people they don't, and they us. It is something that binds us to them, and them to us. All we are is our relationships, as asymmetrical and odd and exquisite as they might be, and the knowledges they form and hide. Or squander.

Between me and Ace, in the muzzled quiet of the prison classroom, was Jakes. The two of them sat on the long side of a table, and I was next to them, at a table with another young man. Class busywork had long since subsided, and chess and conversation were outlawed for the moment. I spent untold minutes considering the sogginess of my socks, the cracks in the seams of my snowboots that yawned widely each time I took a step, and the aggravating cost of replacing them just to live in a city I disliked. I felt fussy, seesawing back and forth between the whole racket of capitalist life and the grief of repudiated mothers.

Between Ace and me, Jakes sat doodling on a quiz he hadn't turned in simply because this teacher would not give him "free" paper for his doodles. Never mind that in the principal's office, reams of paper climbed the wall—sloppy white bricks wobbling up from metal shelves, along with a surfeit of other office supplies he exasperatingly amassed. He was required to make a monthly order of office supplies, excessive and unusable. And his office became a cramped warehouse receipt to the state juvenile division's education fund. Wealth for not sharing. Labor wrought invisible and irrelevant. Accumulation for not distributing. Stuff to hoard. Surplus. A man made into a tiny dragon.

Between me and Ace, Jakes doodled and erased, doodled and erased, while I thought about Ace, his mother, and if I could go one more paycheck with my old boots. No one spoke. Jakes began to move the eraser debris around the surface of the paper, making snowy erased-out images where the side of his fist had gradually smeared the pencil lead during his long doodling. Ace and I stared, in the discreet way one does when the teacher is looking for control opportunities.

Ace and Jakes were born long after prison was done being tied to creating and controlling labor in any lucrative sense. Corporate films and best-seller books do little to explain the forces of their current captivity. They were born into the savage capitalist world

of surplus labor. No less or more violent and brutal. Just different.
Their schooling and imprisonment were part of a crude, reckless-
ly systematized, supremacist management of human surplus in a
shifting nexus of ongoing accumulations.

Jakes rolled the eraser debris across the gray cloud of smeared
number 2 prison-issue pencil lead. His movements formed figures
and shapes I couldn't make out. Once he stopped to scratch his
calf. Another time to very slightly arch-stretch his back from his
slumped posture. We are always a whole world in ourselves, and
simultaneously a person just sitting between two other people.

That just sitting between two other people, that earthly, human
doing of quiet relationality, holds in it a whole world of possibility.
It is the will and willfulness and willingness of life. As much as this
is a story *about* the school–prison trust, it is a story *toward* freedom,
conceived and sustained in relationality. Freedom is not partial, or
for some people, or about my people. It is not a nationalist project,
and it is not only a return to the prior.

As Joy Harjo reminds us, this is a journey, and "the heart knows
the way though there may be high-rises, interstates, checkpoints,
armed soldiers, massacres, wars, and those who will despise you
because they despise themselves."[32]

---

32. Harjo, *Conflict Resolution*, 5.

1. Jakes' Refusal, Squanto's Revenge

> Refusal holds on to a truth, structures this truth as stance through time, as its own structure and commingling with the force of presumed and inevitable disappearance and operates as the revenge of consent—the consent to these conditions, to the interpretation that this was fair, and the ongoing sense that this is all over with. When I deploy the term revenge, I am hailing historical consciousness. As such it is a manifestation of deep awareness of the past, of, for example, theft, in raw form. . . . As such this consciousness avenges the prior.
>
> —AUDRA SIMPSON, *"Consent's Revenge"*

CONQUEST INSTITUTIONS actualized through modes of perpetual discovery predetermine refusal as insubordination. This can take on the descriptive frame of disrespect or disobedience or deficit or disorder and has been the object of entire imperial carceral administrations—such as special education or classroom management—replete with colonial surveillance knowledge bases and university degrees. So refusal not only describes "both a stance and a theory of the political"[1] but also rejects refusal as a diagnosis or conduct. It is a sovereignty. And as we will tease out, it resists the imbricate forces of the school–prison trust. As Vine Deloria Jr. notes, "inherent" in what he describes as the "peculiar experi-

---

1. Harney and Moten, *Undercommons,* 166; Grande and McCarty, "Indigenous Elsewheres."

ence" of racialized peoples in north america "is hidden the basic recognition of their power and sovereignty."[2] This basic recognition draws a straight line to the heart of conquest's apprehension and repression. The state's fundamental recognition of Native power helps map the deliberate, counterinsurgent nature of the school–prison trust. Refusal brings both Native sovereignty and conquest state apparatal reaction into relief.

One vital component of that refusal of the school–prison trust is rooted in Simpson's framing of memory and remembering. It is a memory of the prior, *a manifestation of deep awareness of the past*; a memory extricated from fictive consensus or evidence; a remembering inaccessible to the conqueror; a knowing that taps into experiences of the structures that created the current conditions— warfare institutions (like schools)—of the contemporary conditions created by these structures and institutions that make it possible for Jakes, when asked if things might have been different, to respond "Shoot. Naw."

Survivance and Sovereignty

"It had been a long time since he thought about having a name," writes Leslie Marmon Silko in *Ceremony*.[3]

"Shoot. Naw," Jakes said. And he laughed. "School is school."

I looked at him with feigned puzzlement, for elaboration. But Jakes knew me enough by then to just be exasperated with me. So he stayed leaned back in his green office chair and offered a nonchalant response.

"You know, school bein' just a bunch a people—I don't know— they just tryin' to fuck with kids." Coffee mug stains on the table formed a dirty map of overlapping, faded enclosures.

"OK." I smiled. And, as I was about to go on to something less obvious and less annoying, Jakes leaned his sharp elbows onto the

2. Deloria, *We Talk*, 115.
3. Silko, *Ceremony*, 16.

wood tabletop for a moment, in a gesture of sudden interest or renewed sincerity.

"Like they think they trying and everything."

"Huh, really?" I asked, a little circumspect.

"Yeah. Like they got this idea once to do this circle. This lady, Linda, she knew all us kids 'cause she was like the top counselor or something, you know what I mean?" Jakes noticed me noticing him rubbing his knuckles. He had large hands and long fingers with protruding knuckles—pretty and knobby. But they were dry from the unruly coldness of this winter, and the large knuckle on his right index finger was cracked and bleeding slightly.

"You got lotion?" he asked.

"Yeah, but it smells," I warned. Cocking his head to the left, he gave me a pouty smile with rolled eyes, as if to say, *of course it does!*

"Like patchouli," I followed grinning. And we both laughed hard at that.

Before it was designated contraband, I had learned to bring lotion into the prison, because it was one of those both essential and rare commodities. But I had run out of unscented or mild-smelling lotions, and that morning all I had left was patchouli. Though a favorite of mine, it was not popular among the young men.

I pulled the tube of lotion out of my bag and handed it to Jakes, who squirted a generous portion onto his fingertips and began applying it to his knuckles in funny, small circles.

"So, Linda," I prompted him, hoping to return us to this nascent discussion of school on the Outside.

"Yeah. So, Linda's like callin' us into this room like it's all special 'cause she has chairs in a circle and we—man, it was like the *Spanish* classroom or something stupid. Sittin' in a circle, like they always think they doin' some 'Native peace' thing but they don't know nothin' bout bein' no Indian. So, anyways, yeah, we sit there and she's like, 'Let's go around and say who we are.' We all know who we are! It's Linda and a bunch a us dudes."

Jakes took a second portion of lotion, capped the tube, and handed it back to me. He busied himself again with his small circles.

"Thanks," he said when he was done and sniffed his hands in the exaggerated gesture of smelling a flower.

For a moment, Jakes sat back, his hands spread out to dry on the top of the wood table as if laid out to warm in the sun. But it was winter and prison. It was cold, and there was no sun.

Jakes cocked his head to the side again, as was his way, and took us back to that long-ago, faraway classroom on the Outside where Linda was the keeper of absurdity and power. "So, me bein' the only Indian fars I could see in that room, I say, when it come to me, I say, 'Hello, I'm Squanto.'" He grinned, the brilliance of his irony curving up in satisfied wrinkles at the corners of his eyes.

Squanto figures centrally in the myth of pilgrim and Native interactions, including the childish white story of fantastical thanksgiving feasts—the story that cleverly blankets the lived white fantasy of thanksgiving massacres. But Squanto was also a Pawtuxet prisoner of whites whose captivity marks one origin in the stories of north american conquest. He was a world traveler, a traitor, a double agent, an entrepreneur, a linguist. Squanto is a mystery and what many would call a trickster. A trope and a man.

"I'm dyin' you know, laughin' so hard, but Linda writin' something on her notepad. And later the officer and this guy they brought in to help us *take responsibility* or whatever, they say, 'You know, Linda says you're "noncooperative" and you're not taking this seriously.'" Schools, like prisons and prison schools, are sites of dynamic statecraft, where a young person's *crime is being an Indian*. Cooperation is meant to bludgeon young people into being acquiescent and tractable. But being an Indigenous person with an untameable sense of humor, one that rebuts the absurdity of conquest power and its keepers, even while seemingly at their mercy, is a seditious ideological threat. Jakes' pushback against one of countless performances of colonial democracy (a flawless oxymoron, obviously)—one that was a predictable, proverbial theft of what the state imagines and then charades as Native—was of the worst kind of conduct for a Native boy: *noncooperative*. This is the circuitry and circus of carcerality in the school–prison trust: chaotic surveillance of the spirit.

Jakes laced his fingers together, rested his interlocked fists on the table, and cocked his head to the other side, shaking it slightly and looking me dead in the eye, as if to say, *now ain't that somethin'*. To punctuate, he unlaced his fingers and threw his hands up. But when he brought his arms back down, setting elbows in opposite hands, he noticed his left elbow. He brought it forward toward his face, rubbed it with his right hand while looking down at it in bewilderment, and then looked up at me, shaking his head: "Dang." I was already reaching back into my bag for the patchouli lotion.

"Here. You'll smell great now," I said, to which he gave a surly face.

Jakes gingerly began his funny small circles of lotion on his dry elbow.

"You gonna check the other one before you give it back to me?" I asked, leaning back and giving an up-flicker of my eyebrows.

He started to say something but then just gave me a look.

"You think you funny," he smiled.

"No. I think *you're* funny," I said, honestly. He smiled bigger, and then gave me a teenage smirk.

Gerald Vizenor tells us the features of survivance stories include that they *refuse* the singular colonial story of war and death. He writes, "Native survivance stories are renunciations of dominance, tragedy, and victimry." They are an "active sense of presence."[4] And they are present memories, wounds of conquest that often live in humor hiding in plain sight, as sign and symbol, as unconquerable joy. They might be sacred, private, secret, and they might also be secular, public, known. They are wry and incisive analysis. They are individual narrative. And they are collective intellectual balm.

Writing of Jamaica and particular violent state incursions into a community, Deborah Thomas shares,

> I am interested in what these wounds and memories tell us.... How might we consider them an archive, not merely of the material traces of the performance of sovereignty, but also of the immaterial and affective dimensions of its experience, of what sovereignty feels like?[5]

4. Vizenor, *Fugitive Poses*, i.
5. Thomas, *Political Life*, 23.

We treat Jakes' survivance stories as one archive of his life in the school–prison trust and his collective contemporary and ancestral knowings. For us, they help illuminate the *immaterial and affective dimensions* of *what sovereignty feels like* in the binding contradiction of Trust. They are interwoven threads of time and feeling. They are a refusal.

In Jakes' stories, refusal is marked by an invocation of an archival past, an adept and cutting merger of past and present, and the assumption of a future untenable to conquest paradigms. Without question, his invocation of Squanto was met with carceral reply. And we get the material, psychic harm of that future, as well as its killing intentions. But those extreme intentions are also a state precautionary response to will and to the existence of Jakes' will in a future known through past. His will compels us to consider refusal beyond the response to state reply.

Sovereignty in the U.S. context is the more static and abstract description of what should be inherent rights of nations to self-govern (rights that, ideally, shouldn't and can't be given or taken away as colonial rights are). In this conquest context, sovereignty is sometimes an assertion and an assignation ensnared in recognition. It is the forced necessity of receiving or requesting the nation-state naming what should be a given for peoples; and so is, by naming it, not. Tethered, it is the imposed naming of peoples, imbued with the god-power to unname, and so is, by naming them, not. True sovereignty is the inherent, independent power of peoples.[6] Sovereignty in action is in part self-determination free of permission and its threats. If self-determination is what sovereignty feels like—experiences that supersede the coercive authority to assign or declare a status—survivance stories are refusal and revenge: knowing, memory, and creation. They both address conquest and

6. Harjo, *Spiral to the Stars*; Barker, *Sovereignty Matters*; Coffey and Tsosie, "Cultural Sovereignty"; Brayboy, "Toward a Tribal Critical Race Theory"; Raheja, "Visual Sovereignty"; Womack, *Red on Red*; Wilkins and Lomawaima, *Uneven Ground*.

live boldly outside it. They turn away from parsing out rubrics of agency and toward life-giving acts of resurgence.[7]

"So, Squanto," I said, circling back. Jakes finished circling his elbows.

"Yeah, noncooperative Squanto," said Jakes, now serious. Putting the top back onto the lotion, he looked away into the distance, as if trying to see someone, as if thinking about a name.

> All that's in a name is a puff of sound, a lungful of wind, and yet it is an airy enclosure. How is it that the gist, the spirit, the complicated web of bone, hair, brain, gets stuffed into a syllable or two? How do you shrink the genie of human complexity? How the personality?[8]

Squanto. Two syllables in forced and insurgent transit across the brutal reshaping of a world. Whatever else Squanto was or was not, whatever lore adhered and whatever exquisite details were lost, he was a real and therefore complex human being who survived, among so many things, war-capture and slavery, only to return finally, miraculously, insurgently, home and there find only the ghosts of his entire community. The merciless year was 1619.

The building of empire happens in choruses, not solos. Crushing and unbearable, these grief-filled choruses could not travel across the water from the Massachusetts coast to Point Comfort, Virginia, or back. But their temporal, structural coordination was neither accidental nor incidental, just as the conquest relations of school and prison are both distinct and mimetic across geography, time, and peoples.

Noncooperative Squanto

In Jakes' invocation of Squanto, we heard mournfully analytic, precisely satirical, and brilliant refusal—reaching across geography, time, and peoples. Names come to represent more than a sound.

---

7. Simpson, *Always Done.*
8. Erdrich, *Antelope Wife,* 22.

They carry the actions of people across time and into communities. They form a pushback across colonial systems intended to remove or annihilate the essence of people. Names become one and many. While Jakes' story's structural or legal antecedents can partly be found in the Doctrine of Discovery and racialized, propertied rights as frame and photo of trusteeship, the story's expression proceeded in schooling and its liberal state war projects. Putting narrative form and cadence, embodiment and name, to Simpson's analytic, Jakes' and Squanto's revenge mobilizes a "historical consciousness," avenging prior and present, pointing choral adolescent and ghost fingers fiercely at the unbroken link between prior and present, contributing to an archive of *what sovereignty feels like* in the school–prison trust.

"Education has a transitional function of moving individuals from one status or condition to another," write Deloria, Jr. and Wildcat. "In the old days we used to mark these transitions by giving the individual a new name, a name that would more accurately summarize his or her achievements."[9] A school-name can mark a transition from *avenging a prior* to making a sovereign future, even if fugitive in the present.

"When my turn came," wrote Luther Standing Bear, "I took the pointer and acted as if I were about to touch an enemy." Oglala Lakota child Plenty Kill was a member of the first class of Pratt's Carlisle School. Leaving his family and tribe for what he thought was certain death—what else would white people want with Native people?—and with no concept of school (but rather a rich experience with knowledge), Plenty Kill arrived at Carlisle and, among countless other assaults, was told with his classmates one day to select a "white man's name" off the blackboard. "None of the names were read or explained to us, so of course we did not know the sound or meaning of any of them." When his turn came, the son of Chief Standing Bear and Pretty Face declined to mark himself with

---

9. Deloria and Wildcat, *Power and Place*, 79, 86.

meaningless chicken scratch. So he made meaning of the compulsory action. He made it his and his people's. He counted coup on his vacant white name: "I took the pointer," he recounted, "and acted as if I were about to touch an enemy."[10] In that act and stance of refusal, he transformed his forced-chosen name, Luther, into a symbol of his bravery and his triumph. In that act and stance, he established relations before those dusty white lines flew into the mouth of his teacher and became *a puff of sound.* All that, in the middle of one hauntingly inaugural moment in the school–prison trust.

Luther and Jakes assert their inherent being through revenge acts of refusal. Under the rule of educational repression, they practice *what sovereignty feels like.* And what it feels like is in part the doing of it: making an alliance of the philosophical with the active. Jakes and Luther Standing Bear self-determine as refusal revenge against institutional educational efforts to extinguish agency. Notably, their revenge tactics play on the colonial stereotype of traditionalism and so upend both the current context and the framing of past as antiquity in forging an insurgent future. This is temporal sedition. A name becomes and invokes sovereignties across time.

We've described sovereignty as the inherent, independent power of Indigenous peoples. That power manifests, adapts and adjusts to the totality of Indigenous life. Sovereignty has also been mobilized strategically with specificity for protecting against legal and political incursions on Indigenous practices that define community (the philosophical and ephemeral nature of a group's rights *to be,* spiritually and cosmologically); repealing dependence on federal government and non-Native grocers' sickening, ecocidal, and restricted food options toward self-determined farming and distribution; reserving unique linguistic and educational rights; and resisting rhetorical imperialism, among many, many other purposes. These sovereignties gesture toward Indigenous worlds that defy ontological imperialism or the demands of the nation-state to determine the day-to-day

10. Standing Bear, *My People,* 110.

realities of Indigenous peoples. Other sovereignties are characterized outside direct relation to the colonial state. Simultaneous with all these, sovereignty protects the relations of past, present, and futures, honoring time and its creations.

We understand the inclination toward law as a navigation of conquest, and respect it as one of many iterations or navigations of sovereignty. But, as we will consider later, conceptualizations and practices that imagine the state conferring sovereignty may be confined by a misunderstanding of how sovereignty functions. Unmitigated sovereignty remains untouched by gauche and ghoulish versions and interpretations of and by U.S. law or United Nations rights declarations.

Mournful Analytics

Endless pupilage maps onto the prisoner, not the student, in dominant institutional practices and imaginaries. And it reifies limitless state powers of war. So trusteeship, as a soft term for prison, detention, and captivity, makes the Native student institutionally and legally predisposed to be considered simultaneously the war prisoner, detainee, or captive and the school and prison as rightful sites of captivity.

A primary implement of colonial warfare, boarding schools *came for the children* by functioning as trustee sites of "civilization" through cultural and structural genocide organized along at least three complementary, overlapping trajectories of missionarism, militarism, and maternalism.[11] As many scholars have carefully documented, these trajectories were organized around deeper mercenary goals: brute consolidation of property, future possession of resources in Indigenous lands, creation and control of a scattered laboring class, establishment of european moral su-

11. Jacobs, *White Mother*; Lomawaima, *Prairie Light*; Piatote, *Domestic Subjects*.

premacy, and ideological dominance of western epistemologies and ontologies over Indigenous ways of being.

Children were particularly important to the state Trust project precisely because the possession of Native children was axial in the propertization of relations between the colonial state and Tribal Nations. Moreover, this possession was an inflection point, where war and the private sphere or domesticity met. Those children initially targeted were those from Nations with whom the United States recognized active war and whom government agents described as "hostile." Pratt began his program of education on adult prisoners of war, described by Bishop Henry Benjamin Whipple as "hostages for the good behavior of their people."[12] These first POWs were made the pilot program for Pratt's infantilizing, violent warcraft system of schooling.

The children were brought in as POWs not to a military camp but rather to white maternalism in so-called schools, so they became prisoners of conquest domesticity, quite in line with certain plantation slavery mobilizations of privacy in the United States. Such privatization afforded shielded space in the boarding school system for statecraft tactics such as sexual violence and physical abuse. Child labor, both for its own ends locally (farm labor or school building maintenance, for instance) and for the larger state project of dispersal of political peoples into racial capitalist economies, was a termination tactic constitutive of schooling.[13]

Indigenous descriptions of experiences of state schooling and prison have not been those of wholly distinct practices or apparatuses. Boarding schools were in part a proto-penal institution for young Native people. "The incarceration and tormenting of indigenous children in government and religious boarding 'schools'"[14] mirrors the removal of Indigenous people to prisons, jails, and detention

12. Bishop Henry Whipple to the editor of the *New York Daily Tribune*, in Pratt, *Battlefield and Classroom*, 162–63.

13. Child, *Boarding School Seasons*.

14. Newcomb, *Pagans*, 19.

centers. However, it is imperative for us to note, in recognition of scholars who have done this work and people who lived through this unparalleled experience, that boarding schools did not function simply to unilaterally, uniformly remove and culturally sever Native children from home. "Appealing as this interpretation may be," writes Brenda Child in *Boarding School Seasons: American Indian Families, 1900–1940,* "it also underestimates American Indian families."[15] In *They Called It Prairie Light: Oral Histories from Chilocco Indian Agricultural School 1920–1940,* K. Tsianina Lomawaima details the ways in which students were agentive, collaborative, and insurgent. Across eras, the story of boarding schools is both unflinchingly genocidal and spiritedly self-determined. Our study of them as a carceral-labor educational system is in no way meant to undermine a more complex truth.

The publicly proclaimed end goal of the first era of boarding schools on Native peoples, modeled on the military experimentation on Native prisoners of war, was, as Richard Pratt, founder of the Carlisle Indian School, declared, to "kill the Indian in him, and save the man."[16] *Killing the Indian in him and saving the man* sanctified the secularization of Christian doctrine, afforded white male militaries a demonstration of their utility to civil society, and served white female maternalist movements an exposition of the institutional value of nation-building motherhood outside the home.

In the last case, maternalists worked to support the state project of eliminating Native women through the codified degradation of their fitness for parenting and the utter corruption of their children through schooling, effectively merging white womanhood, schooling, and incarceration. This was a race–gender worldmaking labor by which white possession, again, relied on dispossession and disappearance. To make men of white men, they sought to kill the Indian and relegate him to museums, storybooks, (pre)history. To

15. Child, *Boarding School Seasons,* 27.
16. Pratt, *Official Report.*

make women of white women, they sought to rupture the maternity or parenthood of Indigenous women, and leave them dispossessed of their children and Indigenous futures.

White nationalist womanhood—sometimes referred to as republican motherhood or the cult of true womanhood[17]—consolidated its legitimacy through boarding school rites of degradation, suppression, and exploitation. White maternalism and benevolence were intimately coupled to state stewardship, which found powerful expression through possessory interest in children. Such interests pivoted always toward spiritual salvation as a state burden and responsibility.

Maternalists suggested that Native life was a prison from which boarding schools helped young Native people escape. This maneuver situated conquest carceral schools as the institution not only by which the colonial church and state would continue to converge but within which salvation was relocated. This maternalism precedes what would follow 130 years later in schools and prisons throughout the United States as the school–prison trust took its current shape.

Maternalism exquisitely mediated Native land theft through children, as white women's individual state-based legal rights in relation to a range of properties (income, land, children, etc.) were unfolding unevenly throughout the nineteenth century and were tentative at best. In other words, white women were not understood to be independent contenders for righted properties. Maternalists therefore presented a spiritual sincerity of the duplicitous state and facilitated the ongoing practice of land and life plunder—acts of war—under the guise of altruism. In this way, maternalists served as the paramilitary force entrenching conquest power, acting in service of the state project without the full rights of enlistment. Reaping mercurial benefits from their adjacency to power without direct possession, they were the mercenary corps, the covert boots-on-the-ground in the war against Native children. As with

17. Carby, *Reconstructing Womanhood.*

other soldier-for-hire arrangements, the state as syndicate could distance itself from them while benefiting: if they harmed children or failed at the project, it was on them; if they were successful in their mission, the state claimed the reward.

White women of a certain pedigree were central to the dispossession of Native peoples but not to their own possession (self, land, rights, or other property). Conversely, but in sick symbiosis, Native women were legally dispossessed by conquest codifications of property as individual, individual as white and male, and women as property of marriage. So, maternalism was in many ways the flip side of the coin by which various codes moved property away from Native women in multiple and correspondent directions. As we consider later, this relationship becomes centrally important to the contemporary relationship between state schooling, the murder and disappearance of Native women, and state removal of Native children.

As boarding schools moved out of their first theater of war—what some call their assimilationist[18] era—and maternalism's first era simultaneously came to a close, maternalism pivoted to chastising and drawing public attention to the horrible conditions of residential schools and fell in synch with the Meriam Report.[19] This pivot did not change who was a subject and who was an object in the conversation, and it did little ultimately to change the ways in which a certain class of white women related to the state. But it did do two things: remind us that repressive regimes are fickle and contradictory and surface the ways in which boarding schools were always about labor—resonant across myriad models, from convict leasing to wage labor to indentured servitude.

---

18. In addition to cultural and linguistic genocide, assimilation into a gruesomely violent social order included being used as experiment subjects for the effects of disease, malnutrition, and physical pain; incorporated into a cultural practice of secretive child predation and assault; blended into a brutal labor economy; psychologically degraded and tortured; killed.

19. *Meriam Report on Indian Administration.*

Native children were forced into labor in boarding schools under the ruse of vocational education; this practice of forced labor was so widespread as to be indisputably core to boarding schools' purpose and continued function. Not unlike in other labor camps or prisons, children were malnourished—slowly being starved, even as they were forced into profitable farm labor on-site, without compensation, under harsh conditions, and at risk to their health. Native children were prisoners of war—kidnappees of maternalism and the state, and unrecognized laborers.

An absence of labor analytics of conquest reifies Native people as outside significant labor economies. An absence of labor analytics relegates Native people singularly to antiquity and elsewhere, as set aside and apart socially, temporally, as outside shared struggle around common cause. It exiles generations of Native laborers—from Mohawk to Cedarville Rancheria—from the powerful, joyous, and tragic stories of labor: building, organizing, resisting, sharing. It moves Native people outside modernity and the critical analyses of racial capitalism. By reinsinuating the bifurcation that Native corresponds to land (even if inadequately) and Black to landless labor, this analytic absence enshrines a cluster of related contradictory, bizarre, and extractive norms, such as the one-drop rule and blood quantum. If we refuse the bifurcation, we see the conquest logics in fact cancel one another out.

Through schooling, Native children were placed in the Trust of the United States, Congress dictating their reeducation and subordinated labor assimilation, death, or banishment, while dispossessing, dividing, and reselling their Homelands to white colonists. The dispossessive practices of boarding schools are a blueprint for the school–prison trust.

Though the historical era of maternalism is understood to stretch from the late nineteenth century to the mid-twentieth century, we see its active legacies in the contemporary school–prison trust. We pause to say we see a very complex mobilization of maternalism in the current predominance of white women in public school teaching roles and in the overall coordination of the carceral state educational project; however, we cannot begin to do that full conversation justice here. As many others have made plain, the solidarity white women can have with white patriarchal systems and institutions is racial. As the state is materially, ideologically patriarchal and white,[20] white, female teaching cadres that align politically with the state education apparatuses, that support the repressive function and purpose of state schooling through the classroom, represent the newest generation of maternalists who stand to benefit little but who benefit the state tremendously.[21]

As Jakes tells it, Linda corrals the young men into compulsory space; facilitates a co-opted process, including forced protocols; mobilizes a state-sanctioned cooperation; and reports to male disciplinarians when things don't go as she wants. She acts as a mollifying agent of the state carceral project—one whose maternalism is meant to broadcast state benevolence—rather than as an educator, and she fails or refuses (we can't know for certain which or both) to recognize Jakes' critique as smart or Jakes as a person to engage. This points to the ways in which contemporary maternalist stances rely on students as captives to be disciplined and white women as regulators of moral behavior as a tethered enactment of state war-

20. Lorde, *Sister Outsider*; Simpson, "State Is a Man"; Brown, "Man in the State."

21. To be clear, individual white women teachers can and do radically resist and even refuse. And we're not saying teachers across race and gender don't sometimes take up maternalist tactics, expertly. They do. We are not asserting a facile or total collapsing of identity with ideology and praxis. We are pointing to an overwhelming trend. And that trend is this: over time and up through the present moment, maternalist cartels have ravaged the pliable cluster of mechanisms that form the school–prison trust in aspirational alignment with the patriarchal war machine. The aspiration is hopeful— hopeful for rights and power in a conquest context, which means hopeful for the powers of discovery, possession, and carcerality. Aspiration makes maternalism a kind of zealotry—more driven, more surgical, more dangerous. The patriarchal conquest state can confidently mobilize maternalism because the system itself ensures that maternalists remain nothing but its profoundly dangerous handmaidens.

fare benevolence. Her way is the way forward to correcting their errant ways of knowing and being. It also points more specifically to the confusion Jakes inserts by animating Squanto.

Squanto, the historical figure, refuses *kill the Indian in him and save the man* and so the contemporary mandates of carceral conquest schooling. As well, Squanto conjures Tisquantum, the man: he learned English as a captive but was an interlocutor, not an assimilationist. He was subjected to involuntary captivity, removal, and sale to the Catholic Church: prisoner of war and slave. He was captured later by Massassoit and compelled to deploy his English to negotiate a treaty—his freedom contingent upon it.[22] Like Jakes, he confounds the eager conquest narratives that undergird the U.S. educational project. Jakes and Jakes as Squanto and Squanto and Tisquantum confound the war praxes of so-called treatment and restoration.

Precise Satire: Captivity and White Imaginaries

In Jakes' experience, these war praxes of treatment and restoration feature in part as rhetorical masquerades. In the colonial façade and fact of the state where Jakes was triply confined—to collective contestations over land and life in the barbarous enclosure of legal systems, to compulsory schooling, and to prison—juvenile incarceration was officially proclaimed "treatment," carceral education administered as its primary method. On the Outside, the liberal state bureaucracies mandated unspecified restorative justice (RJ) as a component of school disciplinary regimes. While we are not undertaking a wholesale critique of RJ or even discussing transformative justice (TJ) programs, and while there may be significant positive effects in certain contexts or through particular methods, we consider here what they might signify and concretize in the context of trusteeship—particularly as they signal some historical point of restoration.

---

22. Strong, *American Indians and the American Imaginary*.

Noncooperative Squanto is a representation of refusal—he mocks peacemaking as he performs it; he does not act as a predictable problem but refuses to participate in a relationship forged from and in captivity. Yet his humanity is subsumed by the transactional relationships imposed by carceral educational projects. His humor, therefore, is illegible and also disruptive and reclamatory. It impels and confuses punishment, indicting the restorative process the institution is compelling him to engage. He neither engages nor disengages. In fact, while Jakes and Noncooperative Squanto were subjected severely to discovery and processes of propertization, he/they evade performing containment by those forces. Jakes usurps the restoration—to Squanto, the caricature of the white imagination—as noncooperative. And yet Jakes remains captive. The role of schools in a Trust context means efforts toward restoration for Native students are warfare, as the thing being restored is the conquest benevolence of carceral systems and institutions.

Rather than address the warfare of boarding schools and their active legacies, or turn to a frame of decolonial sovereignty, state RJ programs inherently rely on Indigenous students *trusting* and being *entrusted to* the institutional representatives to *use* them in the state process of rehabilitation or to guide them through forgiveness and contrition. Contemporary restorative projects relegate young people to the condition of dependent and dependence, through which they are required to individualize problems and accept personal blame or responsibility for their actions. Such RJ programs often hijack and incorporate essentialized interpretations of cultural practices from different Indigenous communities, such as talking circles.[23] In such programs, the talking circle becomes a whiteface reenactment of perceived Native identity, what Philip Deloria describes as "playing indian"—a practice that "rests on the ability to wield power against Indians . . . while simultaneously

23. Wadhwa, *Restorative Justice*; Goldberg, "Overextended Borrowing."

drawing power from them."[24] As Noncooperative Squanto, Jakes interrupts the process of permanent pupilage by refusing to act as interlocutor for the institution via himself as a white-imagined representative of Nativeness writ large.

Jakes' violation of the Trust gets compounded by Linda being the symbol of maternal state and private benevolence by which whiteness performs Nativeness better than Natives: white women state educators are positioned as appropriate mothers to Native children and, in the case of RJ, as best facilitators of farcically-appropriated, white-imagined ceremonies. In rejecting the false ceremony, Jakes is rejecting the guise of maternal benevolence—both its hypocrisy and its impossibility—as it appropriates, civilizes, and regurgitates Nativeness back to Native people. Jakes refuses the illusion of benevolence from supremacist paternalism/maternalism, recognizing that state-sponsored restoration is aimed at restoring not to a healed time and place but rather to a historical site of surrender that in fact never occurred. "The term *healing*," writes Tanana Athabascan theorist Dian Million, "is often associated in a trauma economy as the afterward, as the culmination or satisfactory resolution of illness or, for the Indigenous, a promised safety and revitalization from prior colonial violence."[25]

The school–prison trust takes up RJ for conquest healing. In this process, the trusteeship holds Jakes as *an Indian for whom there is understood to be no man to save.* Rather, the human to save is the white-human. As we've made clear, this is not any and all white persons, as whiteness itself requires the practice of exclusivity—the capacity for and commitment to kicking out failed whites, making the scramble for whiteness heinously incessant while snuffing out alternatives. This white-human is parallel to the *citoyenne-homme,* not literally the man and the citizen but the human through convergences managed by supremacy. The human here to save is the

24. Deloria, *Playing Indian,* 191.
25. Million, *Therapeutic Nations,* 8.

white-human, and the conquest project that category represents. Here, Linda. And Linda as metonym for white maternalism's self-restoration, for the resuscitation of the U.S. system of education. Salvation is for the white-human who kills (controls, dispossesses, removes) the Indian. This function of the school–prison trust—to humanize the system and its agents—echoes off countless historical walls, such as when confederates redeemed their racialized masculinity with the implementation of Jim Crow, Jacksonian democracy, and a new era of terror. Pratt's phrase in the contemporary moment is not a charge to call the imaginary Native to salvation but rather a hymn of white-human redemption. *Killing the Indian in him saves the man in me,* says Pratt.

In its contemporary form, in the way redemption is held in Trust for conquest systems through the school–prison trust, redemption is awarded to labor in service and with the imprimatur of the state. Redemption is a closed loop, made necessary by the very conquest, capitalist conditions through which it is gained. Redemption is unreciprocal, transactional, and corrosive. It requires iterative forms of repression, with each one appearing redemptive in the moment.

Willful Refusal

Jakes and I sat at the table for a bit: me thinking about Squanto and names, him thinking about something I don't know. Then he slowly broke the silence. "Yeah. Inside you know, they just tell me over and over, I got a anger problem. That's why I did stuff. Anger. So, I gotta work out my anger ors else I'm never gonna get outta this place."

"This place" was a prison. It was a prison called by another name: a treatment center. A place in trust, of Trust. And the prison's primary form of treatment was school: forced boarding school immune to the resistive possibilities of law. He was removed into the new school–prison trust. He was in the care of a *more sophisticated technique.*

Although Jakes' initial sentence was set by a judge, and was set at ten months, his clinician had extended his sentence without judicial review. Three times. Leonard Peltier said, "My crime is being an Indian." Permanent pupilage.

What happens when a subjugated Native war crime of existence becomes an individualized psychological "problem": anger? When discovered, possessed Indigenous youth "criminal" conduct becomes nondocility, noncooperation? What happens when the punishment for breaking the law is to be subjected to "treatment"? Is Jakes' crime being angry, refusing to cooperate, being Squanto? Is it found in being the object of trusteeship? Is it recognizing war?

Jakes turned to me and said, "This whole setup racist. Even me bein' angry. Like, I'm some angry Indian runnin' around 'cause I beat up some white dudes. They was punks. True. Real punks."

I nodded. Jakes nodded.

"So," Jakes unlaced his fingers, propped his elbows on the table, and cradled his face with his hands, "so, now I'm spose to be *sorry*? I'm spose to ask them to forgive me, and I'm spose to think I got a anger issue?" Questions without respondents or responses echoed throughout our many conversations. They echoed throughout sites of benevolent captivity where punishment was treatment and the supposed pathology being treated, the crime.

He leaned back, dropping his hands in his lap. "Yeah, I'm angry. Shoot." Silence joined us. And when Jakes finally spoke, it was in a near whisper, so as not to disrupt the quiet or wake the jailer. "I'm spose to say 'I sorry I hurt you.' I ain't sorry. I sure ain't sorry."

"Tomorrow I'll bring some shea butter," I said.

"Can you put sup'm Indian in it?" he asked.

Ain't Sorry

For Jakes, one of the clear features of treatment and RJ was contrition. For a Native young person, contrition is structurally built into the Trust relationship as forced acknowledgment of unfitness for self-governance. It is an admission of will-less-ness in a conquest context organized by legal doctrine of individual will. In other words, the Trust relationship in part requires Native Nations to be in a constant state of compelled apology for being unredeemable, failed civic subjects. In war, the refusal of apology is the refusal of surrender. Jakes remains a hostage to the school–prison trust, a POW who will not concede the battle or the war through a justice that seeks to restore conquest's aims.

This derivative construction of Native peoples—as *terra nullius,* permanent pupil, will-less, infantile, of antiquity—is fastened to vast racial capitalist structurings. In her timeless reflection "On Being the Object of Property," Patricia Williams considers ways in which meanings of being human in the United States are made within the "four corners" of the contract. She writes that one of the ongoing features of racial oppression "is a belief structure rooted in a concept of black (or brown, or red) anti-will, the antithetical embodiment of pure will. To be perceived as unremittingly will-less is to be imbued with an almost lethal trait."[26]

Jakes' willful critique of apology takes on added meaning in his context, as young Indigenous people's willful anti-will is always also an assertion of self-determination. Specifically, his assertion is a refusal of the conditions under which there was a demand for apology: war. Apology requires interdependent relationality. It requires a general agreement—arrived at through generative, theorized, communal balances of difference—on the conditions and norms, the protocols and conventions, that preceded the harm. But, conquest itself is incessantly reformulated through an exhaustive, revisionist amnesia that requires a refusal assertion of self-determination. The call for Jakes to apologize is both a demand that he mollify the violent conditions imposed on him and a ransom against his anger.

Jakes' apology would be evidence that he is but a fractional reflection of the veridical fantasies of conquest colonialism. In self-determined life, interdependence, independence, and trust are of a piece. But in the U.S. political context, Trust relationships are exerted over, not engaged between, and produce moral mandates

26. Williams, "Object of Property," 8.

on behavior that pulverize the spirit as they impersonate human-ization. Outside conquest, trust inheres in independence and inde-pendence in trust. Of course, a life free of interference or control is precluded from the school–prison trust or the larger governing Trust rubrics as they stand. Despite Tribal Nations' considerable, long-standing efforts to the contrary, Trust is shaped by dominance and control. One need not look further than the fact that the disso-lution of Trust is the extermination of Nations, just as the demand that Jakes apologize is a steel-jawed snare in the larger hunting down of his ontological condition. The hunting party's aim is to capture his being and leave in his place a colonial substitution—to make a carcass of the essence of the man and reshape it with the taxidermist's nimble simulation. One so docile it can be mounted on the wall with other artifacts of conquest. The apology attempts to reframe his existence. Into a trophy. In this light, Jakes' refusal highlights a poorly kept secret of conquest states: state-orchestrated human rights projects are repressive projects.

> The universal subject of a positive human rights is the citizen of a nation-state imagined within a positive sovereignty. At this point much of humanity remains outside of this positive sovereignty as the stateless, or refugees, or those marginalized within states too poor or too weak to provide for or defend them. They become the subject of a new negative human rights.[27]

Trusteeship is founded in notions of white benevolence as well as a negative sovereign right and a negative human right.

The refusal vis-à-vis negative human rights is an extraordinary assertion of will. It insists on self-determined pasts and futures that simply do not respond to repressive state benevolence. In these in-domitably willed temporalities, the state is irrelevant; it is a brittle remnant on an old battlefield. So the state's counterresponse in the present is, as Coulthard[28] suggests, to manufacture a brokenness in

27. Million, *Therapeutic Nations*, 10–11.
28. Coulthard, *Red Skin*, 109.

Native temporalities—a pathologic and infantile self-destructive fixation, which, in euro-epistemic melioristic ahistoricisms, are made primitive and therefore aligned with the falsely primitivized, or underdeveloped, emotion of anger. In other words, in colonial institutions and ideologies, all nonconquest histories are primitive, angry, pathologic fixations.

Counterinsurgent to future will, the school–prison trust cobbles together a blanket psychological pathos. Yet, in this particular instance, what it reveals is the upending political power of Jakes' rage. "Yeah, I'm angry. Shoot," says Jakes. And, "I ain't sorry. I sure ain't sorry." He ain't sorry. He ain't apologetic, ain't submissive to a negative human right, not abdicating his will to a conquest carceral present. Sorry can never conjure justice from the dust of demolition.

In invoking Squanto as caricature, historical figure, and self, we understand Jakes to be mocking the colonial carceral heart of the restorative circle Linda leads. He refuses to acknowledge, to give life to, something that never was. He refuses the terms of the process. He gives life to what actually was. Instead of saying *fuck the circle* (a succinct and valuable response), he says, *I will do what is real, what was: Squanto.* "'Refusal' rather than recognition," offers Simpson, "is an option for producing and maintaining alternative structures of thought, politics and traditions away from and in critical relationship to states."[29]

Tellingly, Squanto is memorialized in Massachusetts for teaching white colonists to use fish as fertilizer for corn by placing fish around the base of a stalk; yet this practice is not only inefficient but not discernibly Indigenous. Historians believe Tisquantum likely learned the practice from europeans during captivity and enslavement. And, we like to imagine, therefore not only brazenly knew he was deceiving these agrarian conquerors but also hilariously knew it was a terrible technique. The story of Squanto teaching colonists to farm the Indigenous way is rather a story of Tisquantum teaching

29. Simpson, *Always Done*, 2.

white colonists to farm the european way with a Native face[30]—an anticolonial joke, a trick, a bamboozling. An enactment of survivance. It is significant that he does this in the context of laboring—exploitative labor for a variety of masters, owners, and conquerors.

In this vein, Jakes' resistive, humorous survivance as Noncooperative Squanto nimbly underscores a complex relationship to place in the critiques of conquest restoration projects. "Indigenous anticolonialism," writes Coulthard, "is best understood as . . . a struggle not *for* land in the material sense, but also deeply *informed* by what the land *as a system of reciprocal relations and obligations* can teach us about living our lives in relation to one another and the natural world in nondominating and nonexploitative terms."[31] In Jakes' invocation of Squanto, we hear an invocation of place, of the relations of place, and in refusal of exploitation and domination, including through forced labor. Its particular structure and principle of interdependence complicate and enrich notions of land- or place-based survivance and self-determination, as Jakes is by all measures dis-placed. And it is an invocation of time—Squanto was captured, incarcerated, escaped, was incarcerated again, caught between systems between places, always moving or being moved. As a historicized figure, Squanto's condition is always descriptively determined by the conquest narrative. While Linda and the carceral state colonizers would relegate Squanto to convenient absence in a history class (or erase him altogether), Jakes brings Squanto into the present, where he invokes his memory to mock the fakeness of Linda's lessons, her overbearing sense of control, and her attempts at building oxymoronic carceral community. Jakes has been incarcerated by the moment, escapes it, through humor and playful disdain makes other worlds, and is captured again. Like Squanto, he is caught between systems, occupying a liminal space through which he moves cleverly toward self-determination.

30. Ceci, "Squanto."
31. Coulthard, *Red Skin*, 13, italics original.

On one hand, Jakes cannot summon justice, because it never existed in conquest (and yet is a figment of its imagination, of the lexicon of its grammar); on the other, he can summon Squanto and all the real worlds he awakens. Jakes' storytelling reveals to us a historiography. We see him asserting a multiply storied history against a falsely singular one, and in so doing, we see him offering an analysis of conquest historiography; that is, conquest discursively operates on the very definitions that are antithetical to being, thereby producing systems not only of repression but also of bald contradiction. As Simpson writes, this historiography features centrally in the practice of refusal; it navigates the tensions of being, time, memory, and forgetting in conquest contexts.

Jakes' invocation of Squanto, in Squanto's Homelands, was insurgent historiography. Between he and Squanto, we read in Jakes' conjuring the interdependence of time, place, and history. We understand him as a Janus historiographer. As gesturing to the only possible conditions for justice—those that are free of the grip of conquest relationships. And then, we wonder, would justice make sense? Whether a legal or philosophical referent, justice—at least in English, and at least in modernity—is a definitively moralistic concept. It is a calibration concept—one that mobilizes some sense of righteousness or principle of fairness through correction. This seems to hold true whether it is imposed justice or resistant justice. Does refusal ask us to consider terrains, past and future, in which justice is incomprehensible because self-determination is not given but a given?

Such a wrestling with justice is woven into Jakes' historiography, requiring a method by which relationships and histories cannot be abstracted from one another or forged as objects of transactional and hierarchical possessory interests. Freedom emerges out of reciprocity and abundance in refusal of conquest. In this way, justice may be partial and transitional. In the context of conquest, it is both a struggle *toward* and a tactic *over*. It is not the end game. As with abolition, and in relation to abolition, it is a process framework, one that calls on imagination and insists on radical change but has no ideal form. In Jakes' historiography, we discern justice as a refusal methodology that seeks to nullify scarcity—a social condition in which freedom then becomes the capital that gets traded and in which the reification of unfreedom requires scarcity—by insisting on the relations that never were in conquest. Jakes' historiography marks refusal justice as a transitional breach in the school–prison trust.

Similarly, Jakes' humorous, mocking performance of Noncooperative Squanto assailed the white desire for anger. While Linda and the men call him noncooperative Jacob, he asserts that he is Noncooperative Squanto. While he is told he is angry, and says of course he is angry, his expression is one of sophisticated humor. It is an assertive act of defiance of carceral psychological control; refusal and resurgence. And it works because of a salient sadness of context: he is the only Native person in the room. Squanto, as captive, as sole survivor of his community, as interpreter, as legend, myth, human, is always the only one. This condition follows Jakes into prison, where, because he is not incarcerated at a federal facility where more than 70 percent of young people are Native, he is again the only one. To be clear, we don't want him, or anyone, incarcerated anywhere.

Isolated, Noncooperative Squanto begins to imagine a self-determined future by refusing the choices in front of him. Still captive, he produces other worlds of possibility in his humor and his performance of a new and old self.

In *Freedom Dreams,* Robin Kelley ponders refusal through Frantz Fanon and Cedric Robinson's considerations of the ways Black radical revolt draws not singularly from resistance to the material but also and importantly by metaphysical, poetic, and intellectual transformation. He writes, "By revolution of the mind, I mean not merely a refusal of victim status. I am talking about an unleashing of the mind's most creative capacities, catalyzed by participation in struggles for change."[32] Jakes' creative invocation of Squanto is

32. Kelley, *Freedom Dreams,* 191.

a metaphysical, poetic, intellectual revenge refusal, fundamentally catalyzed by his participation in his place-based individual and/of/ in collective struggle for change, against empire in both its monstrous and minute forms. This creative, rebellious unearthing and reanimating is in part *what sovereignty feels like*, expressed through the worldmaking enactment of a name.

> There are names that go on through the generations with calm persistence. Names that heal a person just for taking them, and names that destroy. Names that travel, names that bring you home, names you only mutter in the deep water of your sleep. Names that bring memory of painful attachments and names lost to time and the reckonings of chance.[33]

False Prophets

Indigenous children are taken from homes to carceral schools and prisons and other locked or compulsory sites of caging under the school–prison trust. The triumviral combat mergers of maternalism, militarism, and missionarism continue in the constant making of empire.[34] Expressed in the educational war-without-end against Native children, schools as conquest futures of extraction mobilize restorative captivities as war. The restorative war strategy, a camouflaged ambush through twinned bogus healing mimicries and outright removal, seeks to obscure sovereign paths to self-determined, collective knowledge and knowing, and related healing practices insurgent to conquest.[35]

So-called restorative practices and their practitioners— sanctioned or mandated by the state and carried out through the institutional apparatus of school—are wolves in sheep's clothing, false prophets of stillborn democracy looking to eat the young who

33. Erdrich, *Four Souls*, 47.

34. Goodyear-Ka'ōpua, "Indigenous Oceanic Futures"; Trask, *Native Daughter*.

35. Goeman, "Ongoing Storms."

stray from a docile herd, either by choice or by their very being. Not only do these practices most often blight agency by circumscribing dissent or tension; they also pawn Nativeness for a carceral assimilationist project—assimilation into the criminal. Sorry is an admission of guilt; not-sorry is a refusal assertion of incontrovertible guilt, calling into question the categories of criminal and guilt themselves. While the former is a forced, false confession that a victim exists, the latter leaves a question mark. Sorry is a colonial redemption song, replete with off-time, factory-made drums and petrified, putrefied talking sticks. Restoration cements colonial time by forcing a false past (a delusional archive of imagined surrenders and thanks), even if only conceptually. Restorative captivity serves to invent the necessity of state schooling—an invention rebutted roundly by the many Indigenous educators, leaders, children, and communities that have endeavored to build sovereign schools[36]— and so benevolently threatens self-determination. Perhaps most pressing for contemplating the school–prison trust, it shields the structural pieces in play that ask individuals, their families, their communities, their tribes, their ancestors, and their descendants to be OK with having children removed, and removed, at least in part, so other children can stay, and be human, be students, be citizens.

The maternalist thread of removal and restoration throws the ineluctable but uneven marriage of state and private forces into stark relief on the map of empire. As Joy James writes of racist societies, "state and civil society seem to speak in one voice regarding policing, punishment, and violence as the media, educational institutions, and private citizens are organized to further state hegemony in spite of their autonomy from state apparatuses."[37] Writing quite literally on the eve of the centennial of the Nineteenth Amendment (it is August 17, 2020, as we draft this sentence), we are aware of the unruly tensions that govern people's desires to be recognized and access rights, on one hand, and to radically change or dismantle the

---

36. Goodyear-Ka'ōpua, *Seeds*; White, *Mohawk*.
37. James, *Resisting State Violence*, 6.

system of rights bestowal, on the other. And the sisters they will sacrifice or subordinate or be sacrificed and subordinated by along the way. This centennial moment might serve to cleave commonsense from the analyses of why the U.S. teaching force is so overwhelmingly white and female and middle class—not just in individual identities but, more importantly, in sensibilities, ideologies, and practice—and how its uneven marriage to the school–prison trust works to extend conquest desires and state repression.

One history of repressive maternalist violence and its presence in twenty-first-century schools and prisons emerged from the late nineteenth and early twentieth centuries, when certain white women made urgent calls for their own rights. We see the legacy of maternalism in individual actors like Linda, and the official roles that bring her into schools, but also being perpetuated by the structures and institutions. It is woven into the fabric of schools and prisons. Jakes' refusal allows us to see possibility for fraying and tears; he is addressed as a threat to the integrity of the maternalist cloth as it unfolds to blanket conquest regimes of school, prison, and Trust, to cover and protect a paternalist state.

"We All Know Who We Are"

And yet. All these regimes are just clamoring to hold on to feeble, though ruthless, power. They are provoked by the very being of those whose lives make a mockery of their power. The will of a young man, whose *crime is being an Indian,* whose hilarious brilliance and historical wit defy convoluted removals and restorations, who insists on *being,* sends maternalists scrambling and disciplinarians recording and wardens locking. All that, for a name. For being.

Parsingly astute, McKittrick sketches topographical geographies of being. "Ralph Ellison's invisible man is not really invisible," she writes;

> rather he is an "imperceptible" social, political, and geographic subject who is rendered invisible due to his highly visible bodily context as a black US man: he is "unvisible," inside and outside the novel.... This

unvisiblity became markedly apparent, a lived geography, during the sanitation strike in Memphis, Tennessee, in 1968, when the workers— under armed police surveillance—carried and wore signs that read "I AM A MAN." The workers spatially constituted the meaning of black masculinity, and labor, on terms that articulated possession, repos- session, and dispossession. Racial disavowal is seeable, recognizable, and ontological.[38]

Under related carceral surveillance, Jakes says, I AM SQUANTO. He temporally, politically, and spatially constitutes the meaning of an incarcerated young Native man. Simpson suggests that refusal is used "in everyday encounters to enunciate repeatedly to ourselves and to outsiders that 'this is who we are, this who you are, these are my rights.'"[39] Jakes, saying "I AM," and therefore *who you are,* momentarily, iteratively, refocuses presence by refusing conquest and its malignant Trust.

And that refusal is met with backlash. This is precisely because Squanto's willful noncooperation is the always-present expression of human abundance and freedom against which conquest makes and remakes itself. In seeking to *kill the Indian,* Pratt formed a lethal mantra in yearning defense of empire—an inherently ontologically sickly, paranoid social organization. In empire, with its scarcity, its reliance on forms of death, and its obsession with insecure self- defense, Native children are a beautiful threat. In their very ex- istence, they *are* refusal, as they make futures, as they signal that Indianness has not only not been broken or killed but is and will be self-determined.

Systematically working to break Native children is a flailing and potent effort to contain the uncontainable threat to a crumbling empire. The school–prison trust undertakes this effort in part by imposing false recognitions and mandating relationally degrad- ing Trust. Jakes thwarts recognition and undermines the negative human rights of criminal restoration. He says, I AM a person. I

---

38. McKittrick, *Demonic Grounds,* 18–19.
39. Simpson, "Ethnographic Refusal," 73.

have will. And spirit. And I am not here to cooperate. Jakes' refusal emerges through Squanto, a name that calls up worlds and envisions new ones. A name that says, I know who I am.

Two names:

They don't know nothin' bout bein' no Indian. So, anyways, yeah, we sit there and she's like, "Let's go around and say who we are."

We all know who we are! It's Linda and a bunch a us dudes.

So, me bein' the only Indian fars I could see in that room, I say, when it come to me, I say,

"Hello, I'm Squanto."

Yeah, noncooperative Squanto,

said Jakes.

Jakes.

2. A Name and a World: Refusal Relationality

"Huh?" I looked up at Jakes from the notes I was hastily taking. I'd had the brief thought that I was being slow and making him wait too long. And then I realized the empty classroom in which we were meeting was far too quiet. Prison quiet smelled like old, dead dust.

"Your name. Where you get it?" He was leaning back in a too-small chair, and I had the sudden instinct to say *Don't lean like that; you're gonna fall and hit your head*. My face must have said it, because he popped back up, smiling, all four chair legs planted firmly on the ground. He rested his long forearms on his young knees—kneecaps under institutional blue sweatpants, making the shape of smooth stones just beneath the silky surface of a slow stream—and clasped his hands together loosely.

"I mean, you don't gotta tell me." He was feigning teenage indifference and being respectful all at once. "Saw-bee-naw." He grinned.

"That's actually a funny story. If you want to call it that." I sighed; one of my least favorite stories to tell, but fair game. "So my mom had picked out some horrible, plain name for me I guess. And my dad said to her, 'When I was in Mexico'—he hitchhiked there trying to avoid being drafted, even though it doesn't work that way—"

"Drafted?"

"Yeah, for the war in Vietnam. Against Vietnam. Back—that's

another conversation, 'k?"[1] Jakes nodded. "So, he says to my mom, my dad says, 'When I was in Mexico, I met this amazing nun, this very old nun named Sabina, who was so wise. Let's name her Sabina. After the nun.'" I smiled, but Jakes just sat attentively still, waiting for the punch line or the plot or the climax.

I had to work on my storytelling. The delivery was clearly lacking.

"Sooo, it turns out the nun wasn't really a nun." I smiled with the right side of my mouth and made question-mark eyebrows. Jakes didn't flinch. He just pursed out his lips and squinted a little.

"OK. Cool." He nodded, sort of casually, the way one does when they have no idea what you're saying but they don't want you to feel entirely stupid.

"The 'nun,'" I said with exaggerated air quotes, "was his ex-girlfriend!" I yelled, chuckling. He sat momentarily impassive.

"I knew it!" Jakes laughed, quickly back on those two inadequate chair-legs, the length of his tall legs a forward anchor, planted in gravity's ocean.

"What!" I was laughing harder now. "Dude!"

"Psyched you out." He was delighted with himself. And, for a minute, we both just enjoyed our respective roles in my being entirely fooled.

"But for reals, where'd you get that name? I mean, where'd it *come from*?" He returned to all four chair legs to the ground.

I was suddenly so aware of the specific place and time of our conversation; the anemic torpor of the four walls around us reverberated with their astoundingly infinite, insistent repetition over so much space and time. And, I was aware because those simple, sweet questions also lifted us off the dimensionless maps of the school–prison trust and made a world out of relationality. Who are you? Who are you to me? Who am I to you? Who claims you?

1. Though the american war against Vietnam is part of the same conversations this book joins, we also acknowledge we can by no means rightly attend to it here.

Who do you claim? A name conveys time and place across the deep river of relations.[2]

"Mm. Mhm. That's a serious story," I said.

"Alright." And he settled in. Jakes had that quality of the best storytellers—he could get anyone else to tell a story, to stay in it, to stretch it out, to get lost in his total audience. He was gleam and spark in the colorless asphyxia of prison.

"Well, people tell me the name is everywhere," I said, picturing my name popping up all over a space-time map. "It's in Spanish and in German and some other European languages—apparently there was an airline but spelled with an *e* at the end. It's Russian, Farsi, and so many places, languages, I guess. But where it came from is really a story." Gray wind whimpered through cracks in the window at the far end of the room.

"You know, when the Greeks in Troy lost the Trojan War, they had to leave. Or escape, obviously. So, a group of men apparently sailed to what is now Italy. In the area of Rome there were Indigenous people called the Sabines." I paused for an aside—"I guess they, the Greeks, called it Rome for one of those men, Romulus; at least that's one story"—and then returned to my main story: "They—the Sabine people—lived in the hills around Rome forever. It was their home. Funny, I don't even know what they called it. The story goes that these Trojan men decided they wanted to steal the place and make it their new home." Maps began to form on top of maps. Self-proclaimed men—*man* as human—sailed from one conquered place to another to create new stories and new worlds with new names, or new stories for old names.

Names identify. Names can be overwritten, appropriated, or purposefully forgotten through conquest. Men naming things for men whose names themselves are bereft of reciprocal relationality, whose names celebrate the failure to understand that a name cannot stand in isolation, is the brash marking of cosmologic thievery,

2. Basso, *Wisdom*; Blu, "Homeplace."

an elision of violence and a proclamation of it all at once. "Things started going wrong," as Turtle Mountain Band of Chippewa writer Louise Erdrich reminds us, "when places everywhere were named for people—political figures, priests, explorers—and not for the real things that happened in these places—the dreaming, the eating, the death, the appearance of animals."[3]

Maps and Trespasses

"Because for whatever reason they didn't bring women with them," I went on in my awkward and partial telling, "they decided to kill all the Sabine men and rape and forcibly marry all the Sabine women of a certain age. So, the Sabine women became the unwilling mothers of Rome." Name maps and rape maps and conquest maps and time maps and prison maps. And none of them explain how all of this works together. Yet, "Standing at the foot of a map of loss is clarity."[4]

These vanquished Greeks laid new hemic layers—where perhaps igneous, sedimentary, metamorphic ones once freely cradled time immemorial—on the fecund hills. On Indigenous life. They laid the cold stone of the new story of Rome where the pillars of the Colosseum would be erected, where spectacle and death would be the unstaunched lifeblood of Roman society.

There is no single map of empire. No way to chart its horrendous, dynamic dimension. War is one dimension with so many other dimensions. Balibar writes that, in "the system of competing states," there is "inescapable impact." He suggests, "We find it in the form of *warfare* that has become typical in the era of national states, as 'total' wars."[5] This ostensibly new and *total warfare* overtly maps a patriarchal notion of the history of nations, one in which nationhood and conquest and conflict are recognized through narrow rubrics. In this Roman city of antiquity, the Sabines—as did the women of the

---

3. Erdrich, *Night Watchman*, 345.
4. Simpson, *Always Done*, 15.
5. Balibar, "Nation Form," 336–37, emphasis added.

discovered, new world—most definitely encountered total warfare. What masculinist political temporalities make new so often maps over what women know as very old, indeed ancient, technologies of control: the assault and possession of their bodies, the removal of their collective children, the massacre of their people. *There is no single map of empire.*

And yet, many empires start this very way—with a single, partial map, full of misty, distorted, blank spots and fantastical sea creatures, where rape, various removals of children, and plunder will give contour and measurement to the conquest topography. Where, as in Rome, humans are made into citizens of empire as they leave their mothers' bodies and land hauntingly motherless on amnesic cartographies covering Indigenous Homelands. The birth and death of individuals and tribes commingle.

"It's a heavy story." I sighed to Jakes, wanting to do right by it, wanting to offer Jakes something meaningful. "Don't know why you'd *e*-ver name your kid Sabina. Genocide. Rape. Unwilling mother of Rome. Dark shit to impose on someone for life." A tiny hole tore open in the space-time map, and I wondered if we'd fall into it. Louise Erdrich describes that puncture: "You cannot feel time grind against you. Time is nothing but everything, not the seconds, minutes, hours, days, years. Yet this substanceless substance, this bending and shaping, this warping, this is the way we understand our world."[6] Time is an understanding.

"I guess your dad wasn't thinking about it too much," said Jakes. Good storytellers like Jakes are boundlessly generous.

"No, he definitely was not." No, indeed.

"Yeah, yeah. But like I think it's dope." Jakes kind of jumped up in his chair. "Like, look at this: Columbus is Native. And the dude didn't even know it!" He was deeply delighted, I guess, because he started snort-giggling and tapping his knee with his fist. I was simply

6. Erdrich, *Night Watchman,* 193.

stunned by the beauty and brilliance of his sight; "indian time is a form of time travel," writes Billy-Ray Belcourt.[7]

"I mean, check it out, like, the I-talians, man, they great great great great grannies some Native people. That's some cool shit." And we both fell into convulsive laughter, while old maps disintegrated or caught fire and smoldered or collided and exploded in atomic light. And something new and very old rolled out. A story. Columbus the Native man. The Sabines' revenge. The timeless, time-traveling, migratory everywhere power of Indigeneity. "It was the silence of before creation, the comfort of pure nothing."[8] And everything.

Jakes' time travel is refusal relationality, rearranging dimensions in the spirit of Trickster. For many Indigenous peoples, Tricksters— who sometimes show up and are embodied by Coyote or Raven, or sometimes take another form—create vital didactic problems or render influential lessons, often uncomfortable, disconcerting lessons that upend settled truths. White Earth Chippewa scholar Gerald Vizenor writes,

> The tribal trickster is a comic *holotrope*. . . . The trickster is immortal; when the trickster emerges in imagination the author dies in a comic discourse. To imagine the tribal trickster is to relume human unities; colonial surveillance, monologues, and racial separations are overturned in discourse. . . . The trickster mediates wild bodies and adamant minds; a chance in third person narratives to turn aside the cold litanies and catechistic monodramas over the measured roads to civilization.[9]

In a singular moment of Tricksterness, Jakes' I-talian Native grannies story challenges what many have come to take as settled truth: that Columbus was an *I-talian*.[10] Or that Italians are of a nation and

---

7. Belcourt, *Wound*, 30.

8. Erdrich, *Little No Horse*, 60.

9. Vizenor, *Trickster*, x.

10. Columbus is also an archive of merging european forces. Papal bulls functioned as one part of a network of powers (Italian merchants, Portuguese capitalists, Spanish monarchies, etc.) that gave rise to the Portuguese empire—an empire nation deserving more credit for Columbus's

ancestry somehow immaculately devoid of Indigeneity. Jakes' story remembers for us that Columbus is the descendant of Indigenous women—it *relumes* Columbus' beginning, laying bare an origin story that makes and contains him. And Jakes' story constructs the didactic problem that Nativeness is therefore not a product of fictive Columbian time (because such a time is now in question), and so the Sabines could be Native. In essence, Jakes' story forces us to disrupt the beginning by exposing the *catechistic monodrama that paved the road of civilization*. Reluming is a presencing project and practice, and Jakes relumes a history of the spiritual shadow that was the so-called Enlightenment. Perhaps more importantly, he relumes by reclaiming origins and Nativeness and the power of Indigenous women.

Where you get your name? Relationality inflects and contains refusal and survivance, expressed here in the kernel of a simple question about a name. Where did it come from? What does it mean? How does it carry you to me? Squanto, Columbus, and Sabina are names and ideas and histories. Each has its own stories. Each has its own places. Some of them are contested and contradictory. Others are humorous, tragic, conflicted, violent, and triumphant. They are "a puff of sound" and a world. Names walk with their bearers— sometimes preceding them, sometimes haunting them, sometimes bringing them to us long after the walking body is gone. Names promise to bring us a refusal relationality that crumbles conquest time. Names are always, and forever, relational.

Origins and Empire

Within empire—within all its unmappable brutalities and abject possessions, within its lethal insistence on the divine truth of a

---

ultimate expeditions than any other and which coordinated Italian capitalists to shape the early contours of the Atlantic slave trade. Columbus "embodied the connective" among european power entities that moved rapid-speed toward conquest. He became synecdoche. Robinson, *Black Marxism,* 110.

singular map—is also the inextinguishability and expansiveness of Indigenous life: relational survivances, refusals, revenges, resurgences, and time travels. In the genocidal conquest of Indigenous life is also the infinite map of empire's demise and the timeless possibility of return forward. Jakes tells a story, not of Indigenous life locked in a colonial past of total death and erasure, but as swimming in the ontological and viscous blood of I-talians. Pumping their very hearts. These are diasporas that upend colonial space-time. Relationships that refuse the terms of conquest time.

Jakes' story refashions identities by taking a convenience-store lighter to the flat-earth parchment map of Rome. It repositions historical and contemporary time. "Through imposed spatial ideologies and their narration in popular culture, land and people become seemingly bound and fit into tight containers," observes Mishuana Goeman. "The danger of identities fixed in *time and space* is well known to Native people—what becomes elided in the colonial political bind are the histories of *movement and mobility of people and ideas*."[11] If in Jakes' summoning of Squanto we see an act of refusal—witty, brilliant, and devastating—in his pulling of the Sabines across time and space into Nativeness and Nativeness into Columbus and Italians, we see refusal in motion—a *movement and mobility of peoples and ideas* that migrates the conditions of space and time through relationships, rather than the other way around. Notably, Jakes' stories refuse the entrapment of colonial past-lookingness and land-singularity and bring forward a boundlessness that resists confinement—here, the Sabine women's confinement as forced, vanished mothers of a nation.[12] The supposed end-beginning is always in the present precisely because relationships are the context, the condition, the shape—the dimension—through which time, place, and space emerge, meet, configure, and move. And a name is a home for this dimension called relation.

---

11. Goeman, "Spatial Practice," 179, italics added.
12. Vaught, "Vanishment."

In their recent essay "On the Development of Terrortory," Bryan and Jeremiah write that in "the vanishing Native ideology ... genocide and colonization are presented as foregone conclusions, not ongoing terrors."[13] Absence works to concoct a blank slate—one on which a beginning might be inscribed. On what remained of the inaugural stone inscription on the Colosseum—(a remnant of practices of etching beginnings in stone)—were these words: "Emperor Caesar Vespasian Augustus ordered a new amphitheatre to be made from spoils."[14] The "est."—the inscribed claim to a geologic beginning, the overlay of the sediment of empire—is always an act of war. What were the war "spoils" on which this enormous monument to the most violent relational Roman indulgences were established? Indigenous people, fabricated absent. And absence works to make places of *ongoing terrors* appear as *foregone conclusions*. Refusal relationality rouses multiple presences in place, creating an inconclusive tension for empire.

What, then, for refusal relationality and this seemingly impenetrable, immovable *terrortorial* bedrock of conquest? Relationships of power and domination, repression and race, writes Wynter, "must now be returned to, re-examined, and reclaimed, as the first stage, however then incomplete, of our coming to grips with the real issue (the territory rather than its maps) with which we are now urgently confronted ... to create now our own Word, by separating discursively as well as institutionally, the notion of human from the notion of Man."[15] If Man—Roman man, I-talian man—is terror magistrate and mapmaker of the foregone absence, Jakes *creates now his own Word,* starting in the profoundly reclaiming word: a name. Squanto. Sabines. Columbus. A name moves heavy stone and dusty archived time through the dimensional portals of relation. In Jakes calling names, we hear a way to *relume human unities*.

Jakes calls names, and we hear possibilities to "(re)map": Goeman's survivance-framed method of "spatial decolonization."

13. Brayboy and Chin, "Terrortory," 23.
14. *Piranesi in Rome,* "Inscriptions."
15. Wynter, "Mistook the Map," 161.

Not "a recovery project," Goeman configures (re)mapping as making sense of "the theoretical dimensions of power that struggle over geography's hold."[16] Mobilizing relationships as the primary dimension, Jakes' refusal-relationally makes the Word of names, going not back in time nor undertaking a project of recovery but rather reminding us and perhaps himself: Squanto is here, now, and there, then; the Sabine women are here, now, and there, then. And in this reminder is the relational (re)mapping of what we might frame as the tense distinctions between origins and beginnings. (Re)mapping through the refusal-relational relumination of the name not only challenges conquest dimensions but reveals and revels in others.

What we have come to hear as Jakes' avenging, slipstreaming, (re)mapping refusal-relational story (the Sabines to Native women in the americas, among other relationships) forges an origin story that accounts for empire and its intrinsic demise. How do we think of origins? Are they the same as beginnings? For many Indigenous peoples globally, origins are stories of emergence. From the earth. Water. Sky. For all Creation. Peoples emerge from somewhere, invited or challenged or fooled into reciprocal relationships that span and make time immemorial—a time that is neither singular nor isolated. A time that does not reign over others. Origins *relume* timeless unities of peoples and places in perpetual relationships. And those relational emergences are a dimension through which time and place should move in alignment: the life-giving sacrifice of the creature weakest in body but strongest in heart, sharpest in mind, greatest in courage; the necessity of interdependence—an anatomical reciprocity—in generating futures. Origins and their dimensions are an inextricable, sustained swirl of love, trickery, loss, and giving.

All origins are beginnings, in a way. Conquest beginnings, however, signal something else entirely. They are not, cannot be, rooted in a reciprocal relational emergence. They are a lie enforced as a

16. Goeman, *Mark My Words*, 3, 4.

truth with its retelling and reenacting. When is the beginning of the so-called United States? What is the function of a plaque that reads "Est."? What is a year? A date? An era? An age? How are beginnings weaponized through their singularity, their extortionist requirement to be the only, to erase, eradicate, absent, abandon, and discard competitors? Worse, how do they thrive through their bloodthirsty drive to defile and exterminate coexistence, to posit it as dangerous and vile? How are such beginnings coterminous with ends, and what kind?

The barrels, gaskets, springs, calibers, wheels, and jewels of the watch that ticks off the time of empire move in captive, uniform, unyielding, redundant synchrony. Unmoved by the sun or moon, by seasons, untouched by love or grief, unwarped, unbent, unforgiving, the watch tracks a beginning—*the* beginning—and each fiendishly unwavering second that follows, in an uninterrupted line toward the end. The watch demands obedience and pinches every last bit of life into its confining, unnatural *tick, tick, tick, tick, tick.*

Refusal Memory

As if directly visiting Anishanaabe scholar Gerald Vizenor's characterization of survivance, Jakes' story takes up the praxis that "Native sovenance is that sense of presence in remembrance, that *trace* of creation and natural reason in native stories . . . not the romance of an aesthetic absence or victimry."[17] In it we hear memories inflected with creation and myriad presences. Yet we hear a relation to imagined Columbian time, space, and being, in brilliant dialectic with Vizenor, who writes,

> The *indian* has no native ancestors; the original crease of that simulation is Columbian. . . . The *indian* is a simulation, the absence of natives; the *indian* transposes the real, and the simulation of the real has no referent, memories, or narrative stories. The *postindian* must waver over the aesthetic ruins of indian simulations.[18]

17. Vizenor, *Fugitive Poses*, 15, emphasis added.
18. Vizenor, 15, emphasis added.

But Jakes' story writes all that is ostensibly Columbian a fiction. Without ignoring its abiding brutality or undermining the experience of its ravages, his story also brings it to its epistemic and ontologic knees. He confounds the Columbian as evanescent identity and resurrects it as a lost and perhaps sociopathic child. The I-talian colonizer, the Roman descendant, the Columbian, always fresh from some defeat, is the conqueror and mass murderer, the rapist, the maker of single maps and the keeper of unforgivingly linear clocks—and also the one who does not get to determine time, place, or being. He is the discoverer who is unknown to himself and so is fundamentally incapable of discovering anything. An effete explorer. And, he is the one who is unwillingly, unwittingly ancestrally Native. Not simply Indigenous. Native. In *repudiating dominance,* Jakes' story challenges Vizenor's "post," moving it across continents and back and forth in time. Origins migrate resurgently across time and place. In ultimate refusal relationality, Jakes' story offers the possibility of making Columbian time irrelevant.

It is the specifics of this story that matter in two key ways worth considering for their relation to the contemporary school–prison trust. First, why is Jakes able to recognize the relationship of Indigenous Sabine women to their *great great great great* grandchildren, as he sees it? In part because, we suspect, he can understand Native women as mothers[19] to future nation citizens, both of the colonial United States and of the Tribal. As a child held captive by Trust powers, he is caught between those nations, as war

19. We use the terms *mothers* and *women* in multiple ways. In these terms we certainly reference people who self-identify this way and who understand their role in relation to specific generations this way. We also use these terms to reference groups of people self-, family-, community-, socially-, and state-identified in these ways, which of course do not always overlap. We know exclusions and inclusions occur across these dimensions of identification. When we are describing mothers who were and are the target of conquest assault, we mean that states and allied citizenries imagine Native women as mothers or potential mothers, and the individual specificity of their lives is irrelevant to conquest.

ransom against the power of Native women to create anticolonial citizens, sovereign citizens, dual citizens, and so in effect anticitizens of empire.

Trust in this way is an extortion of Native women, their motherhood a threat to the always-in-crisis hegemony of conquest. Each successive generation is a fleshy, breathing insurgence to imposed absence. Each young person a thrilling divestment of possessory logics. Each Native child is a political, genealogical threat to empire. Each a refusal. Trust provides one apparatus of containment, not of children—in the disembodied, unnamed, extricated categories of law and logic—but of mothers who, as an undifferentiated whole, symbolically and/or bodily are understood to make young life, new generations, and self-determined futures that cross asymmetrically warring nations. So perhaps Jakes could easily remember, could recover the memory of Sabine women as essential to the existence of Rome and as such an eternal threat to its conquest purity. The contemporary school–prison trust finds its roots in the Sabine hills of pre-Rome as much as it does in the Doctrine of Discovery or the Marshall Trilogy.

What we understand as Jakes' memory also relumes and (re)maps diaspora. Diasporic frames in some ways reify conquest, and Columbian time. What if, as in Jakes' world, Nativeness was not only of a "new world" but also of an "old world"? What if it boarded the ship of a Native-descended mercenary I-talian explorer, traveled across the latitudes of ocean, and did nothing to temper the violence of conquest but did everything to make swaths of europe impetuously itinerant? What if this story makes european nation-states squatters?

So, the second specific of the story that relates to the school–prison trust, and somewhat following, is that Jakes' memoried Romanization of Columbus and Columbanization of early Rome unzips not only temporal linearity but also western ideological and social linearity. Or, colonialism's revisionist history and labor's gender amnesia. "The obliteration of the African past from European consciousness was the culmination of a process a thousand years long and one at the root of *European historical identity*,"[20] writes Robinson. That obliteration of Indigenous African centrality to european life, we submit, synchronized with an equal obliteration of european Indigenous past at the root of europe's dominant historical identity. It was, as we've described, mutually imbricated in other forms of thought that were squeezed out—the multiple forms of thought that at one time vied not for ascendancy but space. The thought that won out in europe was not its only and shouldn't be its last. Because obliteration is clumsy and stupid, it leaves behind traces. A trace can be relumed and, even in its ghostly form, can be re-membered and studied. Upon study, the erasure, the obliteration, of the Sabines suggests a fatal flaw in conquest european epistemology: it destroys its own beginnings and so cannot survive.

But we are in the midst of conquest's putrid indulgence and empire's gross decay. So we wonder what we can learn about the school–prison trust now. When european racialism is understood through various dimensions of its internal conquest labor formations, it is understandable to imagine its evolution in particular ways. We wonder if, in addition to those understandings, there is one that configures the ideological and material labors of establishments, beginnings, and conquest as relationally racialist. For instance, while scholars have distinguished Romans and Greeks from later europeans by asserting that those two societies did not exercise or consider racism or racial prejudice in relation to Africans, which is debatable, Romans founded the very blood and architecture of their Romanness on the exploited, forced, enslaved reproductive labor of Indigenous women—a system and habitude requiring very specific prejudices, and ones which wound their way with formidable reliability through and with other stark ideological shifts in european consciousness.

As Robinson points out, that region of the world was rife with numerous contestations of power and empire, including slavery. "For

20. Robinson, *Black Marxism*. 82, italics added.

perhaps a thousand years or more, western European world histor-ical consciousness was transformed into theosophy, demonology, and mythology. And, indeed, in a most profound sense European notions of history . . . negated the possibility of the true existence of earlier civilizations. The perfectibility of mankind, the eschata-logical vision, precluded the possibility of pre-Christian civilization having achieved any remarkable development in moral law, social organization, or natural history."[21]

Among the stunning collection of decimating transformations to knowledge and knowing undertaken over these centuries in europe is the way in which eschatalogical time itself came to be the only time available and that it laid a vast and suffocating blanket over the european version of the world. Notably, eschatology quite literally means the study of the end. It presupposes absolute linearity, along with the values of that arc and its relationship to the melioristic or pinnacle end, from individual to heavenly. "Time catches up with kingdoms and crushes them, gets its teeth into doctrines and rends them."[22] And in this empire of ideology and structure, eschatalogical time is doctrinal time, a fatal flaw that precludes history.

Part of its fatal flaw is that, as with prevailing european thought, eschatology is gendered and dualistically, vertically so. This feature has reach far beyond our purview here. However, for thinking about Trust in the context of conquest capitalism as a function of war, we posit that because racialism in europe's labor formations was gen-dered, and gendering is racialized, these are inextricable elements of the developments that bring us to this moment. And in this moment, while prisons and the school–prison trust are systems and relations

21. Robinson, 86. We note that an attention to racial formations be-yond the limited historical scope of the United States generatively troubles analyses of white supremacy and racial versus political identities within the social, political, and legal boundaries of the United States. The european racism and racialism to which Robinson and others refer were formed and shaped in the political construct of controlling or decimating what might look like ethnic or Indigenous nations.

22. Baldwin, *Fire Next Time,* 51.

of containing, criminalizing, and controlling human beings across gender who are made surplus in capitalist relations, we understand the systematic assault and murder of women as similarly a brutal system of handling surplus. In the case of Native women (who might be raced in a number of ways), this is a conquest capitalist system—a labor warcraft—for handling human beings who are simultaneously surplus, surplus labor (unrecognized in the formal schema), and surplus citizens whose presence and absence ensure and threaten conquest capitalist state and citizen power blocs.

European conquest had a model not only in its racialism, exploitation, plantations, and more but also in its epistemic structuring of its own beginnings: empty lands full of conquerable surplus and essential women for myriad labors. The european blueprint to *est.* a beginning is drawn on a map of Indigenous women. Colonization as we currently know it (an active conquest capitalist world order) is modeled on having women already there, and there in abundance—a resource and a technology. Conquerors have to rape to start. And the start has to be reenacted endlessly to sustain the war powers and the capital circulations of conquest statecraft.

"A Complex Thing"

History itself is a cacophony[23] of contested—and a chorus of symbiotic—narrations and systems. In other words, it is a sensibility of time that does not correspond to eschatalogical, european time. History is an eschatological impossibility. And so, as contemporary narration praxes of decolonization or anticolonialism express, how do they suture or undo conquest time as we currently know it? Central to the doing of refusal is to tell stories that shake up the space and time fixations of both colonization and its resistance, to tell stories that draw identity-making out of the carcass of those borders and onto a dimensional chorus of pliable maps. To guard

23. Byrd, *Transit.*

against the shake-up falling sedimentary to the bottom of the river and clotting its flow, but instead to stay shook. How do they both resist and speak outside of the dissolve of *european historical identity*. These stories find tellers who remember and retell. Jakes is such a storyteller.

Storytellers take your story and make it ours. They give intrepid witness to the vastness of human suffering and then pluck from it the most exquisite sparkle. They know the limits of cartography and the tininess of explanation. From the pulverized dust of conquest maps and the debris of single theories, in the face of unstoppable death, they form a contradictory, fraught, uncontainable story big enough for the bigness of life. That bigness forms time through historical relationality, to actual histories. Instead of the primary time-constructing relationship being colonialism, and its rejection, the primary relationship is *peoples and ideas*.

There is no *retrospective relation*. In its place is human relation time, which need not overtly reject elimination narratives, because those, too, are eschatalogical. If there is a beginning, middle, or end, if before and after are human historical truths (and we're not certain), they are at the very least not definitive. Said differently, Indigeneity defined by discovery and conquest is captive to a singular and supremacist past.[24] Indigeneity, as we hear through Jakes' story, is infinite and connected to liberatory love of peoples. Relational time then upends conquest systems embedded in and tethered to Trust.

The end of Trust from the state, through termination, ends trusteeship by rejecting the relational and simply severing the state's asserted responsibility to Indigenous peoples. But the end of Trust

24. McClintock, "Angel of Progress." This relational/temporal tension is not new. Writing in 1992, Anne McClintock presciently challenged the use of prefixes to the word *colonial* and its derivations as reifying temporal orientation that "reduces the cultures of peoples beyond colonialism to *prepositional* time. . . . [and] confers on colonialism the prestige of history proper; colonialism is the determining marker of history" (86). Colonialism is an effect, an experience, and an epiphenomenon of history, not its maker.

also ironically ends the conquest state—a material, legal irony that exposes Trust as a multiply eschatalogical implement. The individual termination (or sustained threat thereof) of Trust and therefore the Tribal Nation in question reinforces the very real fear of the loss of trusteeship and entrenches eschatalogical time as a fact of relations.

Wholesale termination of codified sovereignty would simultaneously terminate the state, which requires the objects and subjects of its conquest and control for its own existence. This irony exposes what Barker and Alfred remind us: that the United States and Canada acquire *their* sovereignty through an ongoing derivative process from Native sovereignty.[25] Identifying a dependent sovereignty in *Cherokee Nation v. Georgia,* Marshall misconstrued the direction of reliance: a colonial state is not a sovereign state without the colonial subjects and Nations whose forced, coerced, and otherwise-made treaties, terms, and relations give that colonial state its definition. A conquest state cannot exist without peoples against which to war.

Similarly, the state cannot incarcerate all Native and/or Black young people. It would then destroy an imperative system through which it insistently plays out its paternal/maternal benevolence claim, its fascist civilizing and democratizing labor and law agendas, its monastic ahistoricism project: its endless conquest war. It would succumb to a swift vertigo, as its first compass—its cardinal combat direction—is foundational, ongoing rape and the structured innocence of it. The school–prison trust, then, represents the state's inherent inability to be independent and self-determined, its violent reliance on Native young people to make necessary at least its dispossessive maternalism and at most its vast carceral systems: school and prison. To survive, the state must attempt to make conquest infinite, inevitable, and recurring rather than a context or an event. The school–prison trust does this. But just as refusal-relational time

25. Alfred, "Sovereignty"; Barker, *Sovereignty Matters.*

creates a situatedness that recognizes Columbus as both producer of conquest logics and product of conquest logics of the past *and* Indigeneity, it recognizes Trust as both a producer of subordinate relations and a fatal flaw of a contingent state. Past, present, and future become connected in ways beyond a simple consequentialism. States, as we and others have argued, are both brutal and frail; their attachments are designed to fall apart: wither, explode, and shatter.

In fact, conquest time cannot escape the alinear nature of time, as its own violence animates it. Accordingly, Jakes' temporal interventions emerge from the lodging of numerous modes of conquest, extending the irony of Trust and conquest itself.

Tribal Nations are a compounded existential internal/external threat to the conquest state's sovereignty and yet utterly necessary for it and, as such, are an unparalleled crisis around which the United States continues to reformulate—a strikingly eschatalogical reformulation. Native young people, then, are ungovernable future threats and so the targets of the abrogation of only-ever-imagined liberties by the sustained mergers of militarism, extraconstitutional or warcraft maternalist discipline, and schooling in the contemporary school–prison trust. It is within this complex violence that Jakes feels what it means to be human.

In Trust histories and contemporalities of rape, removal, knowledge desecration, labor exploitation, land usurpation, resource extraction, and the most commonplace capitalist appropriations of Indigeneity, the pattern emerges: from micro to macro, mundane to spectacular, instances of violence supporting relational time and producing context for refusal of *feeling*.

One of those feelings—a particularly incisive, useful, and beautiful one—is rage. Wrote Baldwin,

> To be a Negro in this country and to be relatively conscious is to be in a state of rage, almost, almost all of the time—and in one's work. And part of the rage is this: It isn't only what is happening to you. But it's what's happening all around you and all of the time in the face of the most extraordinary and criminal indifference, indifference of most white people in this country, and their ignorance. Now,

since this is so, it's a great temptation to simplify the issues under the illusion that if you simplify them enough, people will recognize them. I think this illusion is very dangerous because, in fact, it isn't the way it works. A complex thing can't be made simple. You simply have to try to deal with it in all its complexity, and hope to get that complexity across.[26]

Trust Reformulations: Savanna's Act

"But every so often the government remembered about Indians," muses Louise Erdrich's *Night Watchman* protagonist, Thomas. "And when they did, they always tried to *solve* Indians, thought Thomas. They solve us by getting rid of us. . . . *Emancipated*. . . . Freed from being Indians was the idea. Emancipated from their land. Freed from treaties."[27]

While rage, joy, and a host of other human affectives might be, in some way, *what sovereignty feels like*, there is the very present, material power of Trust and the threat of *emancipation* from it. Emancipation from *being*.

In this particular moment in the complex history of Trust, we have the sad opportunity to observe the way the state reformulates its Termination—"Missing only the prefix. The ex."[28]—power. Plying eschatalogical time and the ongoing, originary assault on Indigenous women, the state is not only remaking Trust, but also enmeshing it more deeply in a web of repressive logics and apparatuses.

As we write, Savanna's Act—thwarted by a single member of the U.S. House of Representatives in 2018, reintroduced to the U.S. Senate by Lisa Murkowski, a Republican senator from Alaska, and passed on September 21, 2020, by the House—is being heralded as a long-overdue, important government support aimed at addressing violence against Native women. A celebratory article in the

---

26. Baldwin et al., "Negro in American Culture," 205.
27. Erdrich, *Night Watchman,* 80.
28. Erdrich, 90.

Huffington Post proclaims in its first paragraph that the Act will "help law enforcement respond to a horrifying and largely invisible crisis: Hundreds of Native American women are mysteriously disappearing or being murdered."[29]

Reauthored at a moment when local police forces were encountering the possibility of partial defunding, legal action against their violent conduct, and expanded public scrutiny,[30] this Act begins by entrenching the role, value, and capacity of police agencies (which of course maintain phenomenally diabolic relations with Native people). The Act is one instance of the hegemonic reformulation of the police and so of the state. For this entrenchment project to work—for clarifications, coordinations, and communications to be supported—Indigenous women must continue to be murdered or go missing. Indeed, this Act expanding conquest carceral power requires MMIW, just as Rome required the Sabines, just as boarding schools required "incapable" Native mothers.[31] The state uses a violence it not only inflicts on Indigenous women but in fact, as Simpson details, requires to sustain its political cohesion.[32] It then insists on addressing that violence through the very apparatus that ensures that the trafficking, disappearance, and murder

29. Bendery, "Savanna's Act."

30. As we know, this was short-lived, and many departments are now enjoying increased funding, as well as post–January 6 sympathy.

31. We spend this section engaging the state's co-optation of MMIW—a retrenchment of colonial war powers that would recenter the United States even as attempting or pretending to reverse, prevent, or remedy. However, we are mindful of the self-determination of MMIWG2S as people and a movement not only in resistance to state, societal, and interpersonal violence but also as autonomous, agentive, and generative communities. We want to make clear the way MMIW in a conquest frame flattens the systems of violences that are core to the school–prison trust. We remain mindful of the complexities, while recognizing the narrow specificity of our analytic purposes and the limitations of our authorial capacity. For work by Indigenous women on the issue of MMIWG2S, please see Lavell-Harvard and Brant, *Forever Loved,* and Anderson and Belcourt, *Keetsahnak,* among many others.

32. Simpson, "State Is a Man."

of Native women, girls, and two-spirit people is a fait accompli. And in perhaps the most savage conquest tradition, it does so in the oldest of divide-and-conquer strategies. That is, as the world rose up against anti-Black state violence, the state and allied organizations mobilized long-standing forces to devise a heroic need for more policing. We see this particular remaking as noteworthy for its mobilization of tethered conquest systems and sensibilities that are core to the school–prison trust. Echoing boarding school formations, this Act re-members the merger of maternalism, militarism, and missionarism.

Our undertaking here is to draw on the already rich analyses of the state's production of and collusion in MMIW to make deeper sense of the school–prison trust. How is the apparent act of war in holding young Native people captive to a network of state institutions and ideologies fundamentally an act of war against Native women, and how are these acts intertwined?

Eschatology and Revisionist History

Trust and carcerality are legally reshaped and reanchored in Savanna's Act, while the liberal left mainstream media does the concert work of elevating several horribly false narratives of conquest amnesia and state benevolence and justice:

> The measure . . . responds to a devastating situation *in which nobody can say, exactly, what is going on.* At least 506 indigenous women and girls have gone missing or been murdered in 71 US cities, including more than 330 since 2010, according to a November 2018 report by Urban Indian Health Institute. And that's likely a gross undercount given the limited or complete lack of data being collected by law enforcement agencies. Ninety-five percent of these cases were never covered by the national media, and the circumstances surrounding many of these deaths and disappearances remain unknown.[33]

33. Bendery, "Savanna's Act," italics added.

And yet, many can absolutely say exactly what is going on. The circumstances are too well known and terrifyingly visible.[34]

In "American Arithmetic," Mojave poet Natalie Diaz[35] describes the (mis)use of data and the ways american numbers are an algorithm of (dis)embodiment wielded against Native people:

> But in an American room of one hundred people,
>
> I am Native American—less than one, less than
>
> whole—I am less than myself. Only a fraction
>
> of a body, let's say, *I am only a hand—*

The false absence of *numbers* is a conquest fugue that inserts convenient massacre ellipses into time. Why do MMIW matter statistically when Native people are made statistically insignificant, irrelevant, elsewhere? And why now? Each woman, girl, femme— every single one comes from peoples. And places. Those peoples and those places *can say, exactly, what is going on*: the full universe of a life that became a number made insignificant of being registered and recorded or necessary for war projects. That is, until now, as the war strategies shift.

Bringing intrepid clarity to the state's war on Indigenous women, Audra Simpson opens her mournful article "The State Is a Man: Theresa Spence, Loretta Saunders and the Gender of Settler Sovereignty" with "Canada requires the death and so-called 'disappearance' of Indigenous women in order to secure its Sovereignty."[36] Speaking specifically of Canada, but with intimate relevance to the United States, she goes on to link the state's legal determination of Indigenous women's subjecthood directly with the transfiguration of Tribal Nations and traces that determination forward to the po-

---

34. Gilpin, "Rates of Rape and Assault"; http://www.CSVANW.org/; MMIW, "MMIW USA"; Carrier Sekani Family Services, "Highway of Tears."
35. Diaz, *Postcolonial Love Poem.*
36. Simpson, "State Is a Man."

litical sociology of MMIW as a central component of state projects. *Is this what conquest sovereignty feels like?*

The Indian Act, as with legal moves in the United States, was an "instrument of Indian women's legal death or redefinition as subjects of white sovereignty." Through the gendered terrortory of "out marriage," in legally disappearing Indigenous women—converting them to "limited" (as women and wives) white subjects—the state not only bolstered its intrusion into land, intervention in sovereignty, and extraction of resources; it also divided Indian women from one another through the subject differentiation of their children (by imposing patrilineal race and political/racial identity) and kidnapped children from Tribes (by making them white) even as they lived with their mothers.

Across north america, extraction, kidnap, and consumption are mobilized by a meticulous assault on Indigenous women. In ongoing conquest, "this sovereign death drive" of the state shapes what "counts as governance itself."[37] And in the state, governance is mechanized through myriad carceral forms of surveillance, exploitation, captivity, and disappearance.

Since the Major Crimes Act of 1885, the United States has asserted its own jurisdictional/juridical power over "major crimes" in Indian Country—including murder, kidnapping, and the thirteen crimes named by federal statute.[38] Each new piece of legislation that claims to reduce federal superintendence (from the Civil Rights Act of 1968 to the Tribal Law and Order Act of 2010, and now Savanna's Act in 2020) actually requires Tribes to exercise punitive power in the same carceral manner as the state, resulting in a multipronged, heavily surveilled so-called restoration of rights. In short, to receive this paternalistic *empowerment,* Tribes must consent to relinquishing authority and autonomy over (information on) their citizens and to mimicking certain modes of state rule.

37. Simpson.
38. Major Crimes Act and United States v. Kagama.

Through Savanna's Act, the state cleaves to colonized groups to reformulate its power and deftly evade the core problem: the constitutive conditions for MMIW work as a vast network of the state's and allied citizenries' making.[39] In this schema, the state is not only absolved of responsibility for creating the constitutive conditions, the epiphenomenon requisite for MMIW; it is the arbiter of just response and the voice of remedy. Native women are simultaneously not counted, necessarily counted, cut in half statistically and physically, dismembered, removed, invoked for control, vanished for control, and resurrected as the objects in need of noble state intervention.

However, MMIW is structured into the existence of the state—not an act it undertakes on distinct occasion over the *longue durée* of its life, not a cluster of crimes on which it intervenes, but rather its structural shape and action, and so the shape and action of some of its private citizenries and institutions, such as the Lovelace Women's Hospital in Albuquerque, New Mexico, which used the cover of a pandemic to target Native women in labor based on their zip codes. Women in labor whose zip codes matched a master list referred to by staff as the "Pueblos List."[40] Uncertain numbers of Native mothers and their newborn children were forcibly separated, terrorized through land- or location-based strategies.

Whether it is the Highway of Tears in British Columbia or hospitals in New Mexico or streets and hotels in Alaska where white

---

39. Klein, "Survived Abuse." Murdered and Missing Indigenous Women are a group of people defined by shared devastation, and we cannot even begin to record the grief and trauma visited on women, families, and communities or the urgency of remedy. We want to make clear that we understand that state and individual violence against Indigenous women needs unconditional, resourced attention. The approach to that should center the experiences and concomitant histories of Indigenous women. Our hope here is to contribute to a larger conversation observing how this dynamically violent system is connected to the school–prison trust.

40. Furlow, "Hospital's Secret."

men from South Africa can find shelter for murder,[41] these are patterned, organized practices in states that mark those places as viable, necessary sites to terrorize Indigenous women, to practice a particular form of terrortory that surfaces its embedded gendered components,[42] to mechanize the murder and disappearance of Native women as a means to plunder and erase place and sovereignty—not only to establish the conditions for this private institution and citizen work but also to invite this work and then occasionally investigate and punish it as a show of both distance from the bloodshed required for the existence of conquest states and the necessary feebleness, or inherent dependence, of Native Nations. States are not dislocated, abstract entities. Their agents and codes work in, on, and through places and peoples.

The meting out of *justice* in Savanna's Act is a colonial feedback loop.[43] Justice is a colonial, carceral contrivance—a dependent condition and condition of dependence, to make more conquest, more carcerality, more colonial state. Justice in this sense is not an abstract ideal or transitional practice of and toward self-determination; justice is extracted and reforged as a tool of colonial state power that reifies and deifies conquest powers. And this co-constitution around and through MMIW over euro-political and epistemic millennia can be traced across myriad contextual paths.

Circuitries of Power

In a statement to the *Huffington Post,* Murkowski proclaimed, "Today is a big victory in our fight to provide justice for victims, *healing* for their families, and protection for women and children

---

41. *AP News,* "The Latest."

42. Brayboy and Chin, "Terrortory."

43. Jeremiah Chin, "Red Law, White Supremacy: Cherokee Freedmen, Tribal Sovereignty, and the Colonial Feedback Loop," *John Marshall Law Review* 47 (2014): 1227–68.

across the nation."[44] Broken mothernness (a fiction of the state, foreshadowed by inaugural rape and maternalist movements, a narrow, controlling stand-in for already-narrow womanness: a womb; a reproductive body; a mother of a nation) is an axis of the school–prison trust. And state-sponsored *healing* is a carceral, missionaristic mechanism, an implement in the ongoing war in which *they are coming for the children* as a new formulation of inaugural rapes. MMIW must continue for there to be the children of MMIW to protect and heal. But these are not girl-children, who might also be murdered or disappeared. They are completely absent from this formula.

In and across this circuitry of power, the incarceration of Native boys is a signal way in which a conquest nation organized through property relations can claim itself by incorporating sustained sexual assault as a healing practice. Native boys are imagined in this new phase of war as in need of protection—into the maternalist and militarist institutions charading as if designed for child protection: child services, schools, juvenile "treatment" centers, foster care. And they are imagined as lucky for this removal, as they are also maintained as inherently criminal, incapable, uncivilized, and violent offspring of broken mothers. MMIW as the impetus for escalated policing relations and infrastructure are necessary for the continued war against Native boys through mechanisms of state protection.

To legibly lay claim to any recognized rights or resources, or to accept imposed rights in resources in order not to be terminated, Nations that are in a state of perpetual pupilage vis-à-vis their imposed entrustedness to the United States must first partially concede Native women as undifferentiated property and must accept these imposed alliances for the supposed protection of human property—alliances that cement Trust powers through expanded, knitted carceral infrastructure. "For most of American legal history,

44. Bendery, "Savanna's Act," italics added.

rape was framed as a *property* crime perpetrated against men."[45] In Savanna's Act, this propertization continues, cementing Trust and the wardship of boys. Women are disappeared so property can be made present, and women are disappeared by being made property. The Act enshrines imagined man-state labor through expansion of policing relations, moving people along gendered dimensions of surplus, labor, product, and possession. It is the exuberant fusion of property and discovery.

The phenomenon of MMIW is also meant to suggest something about Indigenous women fit to be (sexually violently) missing and murdered, which in turn affirms their concocted unfitness to be mothers—an iteratively concocted unfitness essential to the removal of children to boarding schools and the removal of children into the school–prison trust. The murder and disappearance of Indigenous women—inflected with rape both on the individual body and writ large—is fundamental to the conquest-authored, fictive brokenness of Native women and, by extension, Native Nations. Women, positioned as mothers of nations, must be broken for nations to be broken, for nations to be dependent and in a state of permanent pupilage. By its nature as an ideological enactment of conquest, Trust has to be (re)created with nations and with children.

But as with all repressions, the murder and disappearance of Indigenous women cannot be total and be effective. It requires women who do not disappear to make disappearance seem abnormal to colonial values, citizens, and governance (and so, again, something peculiar to Indigenous women). Evidentiary of this is that we cannot point to a policy, as there is not a single, dedicated one, and in fact cannot even reference a name for this practice, as it is well hidden in conquest relations. And Savanna's Act consolidates this by co-opting MMIW for carceral expansion, by using the phenomenon it makes as the object of its remedy. This type of co-

45. Deer, *Beginning and End of Rape,* 17. And, we might add, only those men capable of owning property—originally codified, but still in the dominant imagination as white, landowning, heteronormative, and so on.

optation is counterinsurgent imperialism and allows the conquest state to evade naming its own design. Moreover, it reveals the very present spectacle of absence the state generates in MMIW. But this maneuver is also very specific to gender. It relies on the privacy, secrecy, and invisibility that are the hallmark of violence against women. By co-opting MMIW for the most patriarchal of efforts, the state declares its misogynist, femicidal conquest efforts. This witless declaration indicates the second reason the disappearance of Indigenous women cannot be total to be effective: the state and its corroborating citizens must maintain present women against whom they can enact the twinned and ongoing practice of removal through school–prison trust mechanisms. The school–prison trust is a carceral-as-healing removal of children as property to maintain their mothers' necessary unpropertying rape and murder—original, current, and future.

Since long before the Sabines met Roman desecration, children have been systematically focal to conquest nation-making. In fact, nations are built and maintained through the creation of children who will become citizens and noncitizens, free and unfree. Nation-states, however, are confounded by persistently unsurrendered children. They endeavor to make them unfree over and against the fact that the refusal inherent in their unsurrendered condition makes the effort to corral them into the dichotomy of freedom/unfreedom unresolvable and destabilizes conquest sovereignty. The statecraft creation of unfree children is among the most powerfully sinister praxes of total community control and is both predictable and irregular—fed by the immediate desires and crises of the particular conquest state. In this way, among others, the school and the prison are sites in the same network as highways, hospitals, and hotels. If one cannot be assimilated into unfreedom, one will be vanished into unfreedom.

Our point here, with Simpson and others, is that the murder and missing of Indigenous women is not an aberrational pattern or disproportionality. Rather, it is as determined a system as state-issued scalping bounties or child removal. The murder and missing of Indigenous women as state policy is an iterative, nimble coordination among the murdering state and *its citizens,* who *can do that for it,* and, in that spirit, scoop up the children of women who are missing and murdered or might be or are understood as fit to be.

The U.S. theater of this war is specific. If the children of the Sabines weren't Roman, the women were disappeared. And when their children were Roman, the women were disappeared. They were absorbed as a means of ceasing their existence. Under american Trust, law sustains the nation-state, while school sustains the mask of benevolence in an endless war. So, unlike the Sabines, Native women in the United States cannot exist and cannot cease to exist. Cannot make Native children and must make Native children to be captured, incarcerated, and tortured. Schools need MMIW and need Native women. These contradictions form the sovereignty of the United States, and the school–prison trust ensures that the contradictions are never settled.

However, it's not quite as easy as saying MMIW are the flipside of maternalists. Not quite as easy as saying contemporary maternalism—or a nationalist role for professional white motherhood—requires the absence or concocted brokenness of Native women. True, school itself is a morality war project that constantly reestablishes the conquest state in reliance on the conquest of Native women. Something of *a more sophisticated technique* is happening here. Making Native women's children protected wards or criminals through the imposed resource of policing as protection for a nation's women (as property innately disappearable and unprotected through self-determination—otherwise, why use colonial policing?) not only allows the maternalist, militarist state to succeed in a vicious mission of protection; it also positions its war as a necessary, civilizing response directly to Native women. In other words, this state arrangement blames Native women for the war on their children.

The war in the form of the school–prison trust is retaliation for making generations of unsurrendered children. The school–prison trust is a war machine and a maternalist military prison for the insurgency of unsurrendered children. They are prisoners of that very long war, whose start predates the Sabines, which has been fought across contexts, uninterrupted and largely invisibly, and which catalyzes and confirms the conditions for the murder and disappearance of Native women.

Here we see also that Native women are terrifically threatening to the colonial state. Native women living and raising Native children highlights the failure of the school–prison trust both in its assimilation efforts and purposes and in its genocidal efforts and purposes. Despite the war, Indigenous women are living unsurrendered, self-determined lives.[46] State violence is counterinsurgent to perceived threats. The intensity and scale of counterinsurgency are measures of the felt threat. The state's murderous citizen bond is a counterinsurgent movement against the insurgent threat that Native women pose in their very being.

The potency of that threat cannot be understated. This insurgent threat derives from Native women understood as mothers of self-determined generations, as mothers of sovereign Nations, and moreover (even if denied) as mothers of Nations who confer sovereignty to the colonial nation. This understanding is a foundational threat to conquest, which secretly understands its own generations as necessarily the human products of inaugural rape, ensuring control of place and land. Indigenous motherhood—again, individual and collective, familial and national, bodily and political—that is not catalyzed by colonial rapes—interpersonal and structural, contemporary and historical—is unmitigated in-

46. There is extensive scholarly and creative work by and about Native women from which our narrow project of beginning to map the school–prison trust draws but cannot represent. For further reading, see the work of Kate Shanley, Joanne Barker, Heather Shotton, Amanda Tachine, Mishuana Goeman, Paula Gunn Allen, Beth Piatote, Gretchen Bataille, Kim TallBear, Tsianina Lomawaima, LeAnne Howe, Cherie Dimaline, Jennifer Nez Denetdale, Leslie Marmon Silko, Cutcha Risling Baldy, Jodi Byrd, and many others.

surrection. Thus, Native women's murder and missingness is a maintenance of the conquest nation.

Sedition

Against undefeated, unsurrendered peoples, acts of Congress are acts of war. Often these acts take the form of antimemory ordnance, decimating histories to make new ones. Savanna's Act asserts surveillance and law over people in the amnesic attention to missing and murdered Indigenous women, an act of war designed to rewrite the story by making it instead an act of nature or an act of god or an act of social deviance. But most tellingly, a private act. By assuming colonial frameworks for sexual violence—as private, individual, pathological—acts (VAWA, the Violence against Women Act, for instance) are able, in their very assertion, to shield what is an act of war. Conquest is hidden, entrenched, and amplified.

The specificity of this particular act of war matters too. It links to gender contestations fastened to the school–prison trust. Matrilineality means little if its governance is patriarchal, patrilineal, neocolonial nationalism, of any or multiple sorts. Trust encourages nation-to-nation dynamics that can rely on misogynist governance, law, and ideology—nations can be invested in the divestment, control, and dispossession of Native women in this framework.

Examples of MMIW as a function of Trust by which some Native women get caught between (extremely unevenly powered) nations are everywhere. One might look at the case of Carmen Tageant, a Nooksak member who was at one point a domestic violence advocate and also a Tribal Council member and whose disenrollment involved complex histories of quantum, census, Trust, resource scarcity, labor competition, and allotment, but were enacted through public sexual harassment and shaming, gendered online abuse, loss of employment, and anti-Filipino racism.[47] Carmen Tageant was

47. Hu, "Disenrollment."

"dismembered,"[48] disenrolled as a tactic to cut her off from life and limb. It is noteworthy that dismemberment is a practice of femicide. Women are dismembered. Just do a Google search. It is grisly global normativity. The dismemberment of women through disenrollment, exile, banishment, captivity, and otherwise loss of citizenship writ large, particularly as political retaliation scaffolded onto severe sexual harassment and assault, is normal—not aberrational—to contemporary nationalism.

A group of Tobique women who had formed several decades ago to "improve local living conditions for women and children" ultimately organized to dismantle the century of violence engendered by the Indian Act. Mavis Goeres, among their members, said the following of their conditions and their self-determination: "We all knew that no government agency—be it white or be it Indian—was going to tell us we were no longer Indian, when we *know* we are Indian."[49]

Not only did Indigenous women suffer disenrollment through an act of war and its shared enforcement across nations; they were also constitutively banished from the collective decision over who makes a community. This wholesale dismemberment, whether or not an individual retains enrollment, is an embargo on being—a very core, private, ontologic disappearance. It has long been the privatization of structural combat against Native women that bricks the armory of the school–prison trust.

In the conquest history of what is called north america, Native children were not only removed as prisoners of war against their mothers and tribes; Native mothers were not only targeted as unfit by military-maternalist orgies of counterinsurgent domination; Native women are not only the targets of the sickening sexual violence and shocking femicidal drives. They also lived at the center of one of the state's comprehensive racial capitalist experiments,

48. Wilkins and Wilkins, *Dismembered.*
49. Silman, *Enough,* 9.

shielded by the intense gendered privatization strategies of conquest. For instance, some Native women sent their children to residential schools because the collision of "ecocidal" devastation by
timber "cartels," combined with racism in local schools, layered on
the widowing devastation of disease emboldened by dilapidated
health care, enacted through relegation to reservations and their
subjection to poverty, merged with the devastation of seasonal food
economies, collapsed with allotments, amplified by fraud and star-
vation, coupled with coerced and compelled movement into urban
areas and houselessness, and entrenched by domestic violence and
paternal abandonment, drove Native women into wage labor. This
wage labor caused such great poverty that one individual and policy
solution was residential schooling, at which children were ostensibly trained in vocational skills—often by doing labor—for further
destitute wage labor. "It was widely assumed that vocational education not only suited the 'native mentality' but would also help to
solve the nation's so-called 'Indian problem' by training the growing
number of impoverished and landless Indians for wage labor."[50] And
yet, because that schooling was residential, it was absorbed into the
dominant privacy framework and sensibilities of domestic, familial
life. This ideology and structure of the residence merged subjugated
wage labor, domestic violence, and schooling.

The thrust for wage labor and its ensuing cycle of impoverishment in a devastated conquest context defined a powerful iteration
of residential schooling—one that contributes an important blueprint layer for today's school–prison trust. But it also shows how
labor, not only land, is a fundamental and gendered analytic for the
school–prison trust. The absenting of labor from the central historical analysis of colonization (and its de-) contributes to a presence
in which Indigenous women, in particular, are recognized saliently
as bodies, as of nature, and as outside the intensive wage, enslaved,
indentured, itinerant, migrant, and convict labor that built vast ar-

---

50. Child, *Boarding School Seasons,* 13.

eas of what is called the United States. Native women pressed into labor is part of a widespread conquest pattern. For instance, in 1953, Congress passed HCR 108, which terminated 109 tribes. Aspects of removal were tied to labor in the bill. Native people received one-way bus tickets to urban areas across the United States, with promises of well-paying jobs. Once removed, they found low-wage jobs or no jobs, with no way to return home. The confluence of land and labor extraction and exploitation is pronounced, profound, and persistent. Moreover, a rigidly limited, polarizing imagining of Native women relegates what can be dominantly imagined of their labor to conscripted sex work.

The all too familiar trope of a singular focus on land as it relates to Indigenous peoples elides the role of labor in the equation. Extraction drives part of the story. Extracting timber, or gas, or uranium, or coal required not just land from which to take it but also laborers, who would be left with little option but to engage in the high-risk, low-wage work. Land and labor are twinned extraction and exploitation. Removal of peoples and things on and in lands. Boarding or residential schooling was a cost of that labor, a taxation on Native women. And when wage laborers were made surplus, we know that prison expansion mushroomed.[51]

In the contemporary era of mass surplus labor, Native women are dominantly imagined outside precarious, conquest capitalist economies and so a threat to their very logics and organization. With or without a role in these economies, and despite centuries of assault, Native women have and make self-determined alternatives. What happens when people live aware that conquest capitalism is a contrivance, even if they're unable to escape it?

The effort to make the conditions for Indigenous women's suffering is extraordinary. Native motherhood, individual and collective, is conquest sedition.

---

51. One of the ways Native women in the U.S. go missing and murdered is to be incarcerated in both state and federal prisons, the latter owing often to nation-to-nation relations and causing a removal far from home.

Why does all this matter? We are not writing a book about MMIWG2S or about the complex gender politics of Tribal enrollment. But in a way we are. When women's citizenship, legal and ontologic, is contingent and threatened, when their very being in an era of advanced racial nationalism and ongoing conquest is always at the will of the sovereign, always in question, and variously an object of war, their children—imagined and real, individual and collective—become proxies for an abject control. Understanding the complex assault on Native women over time and their resistance to it maps the road to the current school–prison trust.

It is a conquest counterinsurgency entangled with and undergirding the school–prison trust, illuminating the ways in which the incarceration of young Native people is a tentacle of the same beast that murders and makes missing their collective mothers. Refusal relationalities and their shared memories and temporalities do not mitigate the bloodthirsty, ruthless impact of Trust, but they do *relume human unities.* They do disclose the lies of Trust. They do reveal that brute force is never smart and only pretends to be through the revisionist, monastic ideological histories, short and long, that support its regime. Trust is perhaps only a *more sophisticated technique* through the violent accidents and deliberate acts that are the hallmark of white supremacy and its clumsy claims to hindsight strategy.

Refusal memory is a practice of self-determination, the making of a world and a word. Refusal memory assumes that time is an agentive subject, one that travels through us, not we through it. Our relationships give it sanctuary and form and welcome it to our intimacies. What enlivens time is the movement of people and ideas. Relational time takes their shape. Conquest time is anchored leaden to conquered place (est. dates, names, inaugural rapes, soundtracks, and monuments), paternalism, patriarchy, and patriotism constituting the *parens patriae* of Trust.

One day when we're all gone
    and you think we've disappeared.

You'll realize we were stolen. The earth
   will continue to split herself open in mourning.

   The morning sun will no longer rise because you failed
to protect those who are so powerful they're in sync with the moon.

   And soon, hurricane, tsunami high waves will cover the land
in the water you didn't care to protect because

you thought oil was more precious than life.
   —TANAYA WINDER, *"We Were Stolen"*[52]

52. Winder, *Why Storms,* 17.

3. Slipstream Shuffle

THE OUTER BANDS of the hurricane were moving in over all of us. Beautiful white feathers from a satellite, they were in reality gusty scouts, marking a path for decimation, alerting everyone on the ground too late.

Inside the prison social studies classroom, no one was the wiser. The unpredictable, angry banging of the radiator hoarded the soundwaves for itself. The windows, set back behind metal bars and full of whistling leaks, were also covered with a jaundiced, chipping layer of metal mesh veneer. The veneer's small, peeling apertures onto the Outside were grimy and no match for the scope required to see the enormity of a coming hurricane.

The social studies teacher, Roy, got excited by the memory of the morning news and interrupted a fierce chess match to boyishly exclaim, "Guys! So, guys, there's a hurricane making landfall tonight. I'll be at home watching the game, but you will all be here." He was the worst kind of coward.

The young men turned from their match, almost as one, and stared at him, in collective wonder about what even to say or not.

Then, possessed by his indomitable wit, Jakes jumped up and assumed the open space in the classroom, right in front of Roy's desk. (A large, heavy, metal bureau Roy almost never left. Whether sitting behind, leaning against, standing in front—it was his base in a game of white-teacherman-scared-of-the-young-men-of-Color.

His *teacherdesk*: his lonely, spiteful circle of wagons; his plantation and his fortress and his frontier; his panoptic lookout.)

"A hurricane? Naw, not a hurricane!" Jakes feigned seriousness. "Bro," he said, shaking his head at Roy.

Jakes spread his feet, in knock-off Nike slides, easily three feet apart, his too-big, white socks hanging off his toes and heels. He shook his long, gangly legs as if loosening up and situated his pants.

"Roy, I got a dance for the hurricane."

He turned to us. "Yo, Game, hit it." And Game, who was always slow to catch on, for some reason caught on right away and began air-DJing, moving the record back and forth on the invisible turntable. We could all see it, clear as day.

Jakes started with his arms, then his feet. And we all started laughing. Amani, cry-laughing and nearly doubled over, said, "Dude, that's the dopest, funniest shit I seen in for-*ever*." It was a moment of uncontainable joy.

Roy, ever uncomfortable, asked, "What is it?"

Quickly, Jakes paused, legs in position. He stared wide-eyed at Roy. Solemnly, he placed his hands in an X across his chest, lowered his brow as far as possible, and lifted his chin slowly and slightly. "My ancestor, Squanto, invented it special for the pilgrims, to help them fight *hurr*icanes." Jakes paused for emphasis and flickered his eyebrows up as he set his eyes in an even deeper lock with Roy's.

"He called it 'The Cupid Shuffle.'"

And then, to the joyous chorus of unstoppable sobbing laughter and lyrics, he broke into the best Cupid Shuffle I've ever seen, before or since.

Squanto and the Dance-Off

"Refusal is a symptom, a practice, a possibility for doing things differently, for thinking beyond the recognition paradigm that is the agreed-upon 'antidote' for rendering justice in deeply unequal scenes of articulation."[1] Jakes did not seek himself in Roy's gaze. He blurred Roy's gaze. And then directed it into crisp focus. Certainly he refused the unequal lock of Roy's cowardice and of Roy's threat. He refused fear of the imminent and inevitable, guaranteed in the coming of the behemoth storm and life in the school–prison trust. And he refused Roy's authority over those. Powerfully, he refused Roy's conquest assumption that he alone could shape truth and feeling, knowledge and its denial. That he could determine the terms of the debate,[2] or that there would even be a debate.

Jakes made Roy a pitiful, weak, and frightened pilgrim, a foolish audience, and a total outsider. Counting coup on Roy, Jakes turned Roy's gaze back on himself. Roy was the subject of his own derision, a subject that withered against the Cupid Shuffle. He did not ask Roy to recognize him, or Squanto, or Indigenous life. "An enemy has to be defeated in battle, but an adversary's different. You must outwit an adversary. So you do have to know them very well."[3]

In the Cupid Shuffle, the pilgrims and plimoth plantation cower, if even for a moment. Jakes creates community—of joy, expression, knowledge—and banishes Roy from it. He recognizes himself, and Squanto, Game, and the other young men, and refuses Roy, an agent of the carceral conquest state.

But what exactly or how exactly did Jakes do what he did? What does refusal feel like? We start with joy, because the mockery was at its apex a hilarious, creative celebration deliberately crafted for collective freedom that, in prison, is insurgently eruptive in character. It was a particularly dazzling mockery, because in it Jakes marshaled a caricature lodged deep in the colonial psyche, anticipating and recalling the worldmaking ideology of the school–prison trust.

"The indigenous inhabitants of North America," states Louis Owens, "can stand anywhere on the continent and look in every

---

1. Simpson, "Ruse of Consent," 12.
2. Lyons, "Rhetorical Sovereignty."
3. Erdrich, *Night Watchman*, 276.

direction at home usurped and colonized by strangers who, from the very beginning, laid claim not merely to the land and resources but to the very definition of natives."[4] As Jakes stands in a prison classroom and looks into the face of the teacherman, who, with Linda and myriad schooling others, *lays claim to the very definition of Natives,* he mocks Roy with the fatuousness of his own racism, his own fear, his own threat. He illuminates the banalities conquest agents inhabit. He frightens Roy in the full freedom of his comic joy and his command of us, who laughed and sobbed—then and now—in part by calling on ancestors, merging the real and the white imagination, and so stealing back what Roy thought he knew as a thief by trade and by tradition. Jakes' refusal was a hurricane of force, irony, and humor.

In some instances, to command the attention of those in power, to resist, refuse, or convey, a Native person might step into the mask and enact the Indian constructed by america.[5] Might pose as the fake, the Edward Curtis Indian. In this instance, Jakes interweaves the fake with the real, dancing an act of refusal that is both a "social mirror," as artist Gregg Deal said to describe his own performance piece *The Last American Indian on Earth,*[6] and a free expression.

Multiplicities

Jakes was also refusing-as-creating something else entirely. Everyone thought Jakes was Black. He was Black. And he was Native. And everyone thought so. At least, the young men did. He was Native and he was Black. And, a "lilbitta some kinda white somewhere in me." That's all nothing new or surprising or unusual.

---

4. Owens, "As If," 14–15.
5. Shanley, "Love and Read"; Fanon, *Black Skin.*
6. Deal, in "The Last," suggests that in fact he had to do very little but walk around public places or stand wearing costume-like, Made-in-China fake regalia, and it was non-Native people who performed in relation to him. There is a rich, long conversation about performance and colonialism. Khubchandani, *Ishtyle*; Muñoz, *Disidentifications*; Mercer, *Travel and See.*

But there was a rupturing dimension to what he said. He was not seeking recognition from anyone and yet from many, but on self-determined terms: "Why I gotta pick? Like, why do these fucki— ooh, oops, sorry! Why everybody think like you Black with a Indian granny or you Indian and your people got up with some slaves or sup'm. Like, what is you, really?" And his *really* was multiple and synergistic. He described himself as recognizably physically and aesthetically "Indian"[7] and, without contradiction, as similarly Black. He identified with communities, cultural practices, politics, ancestries.

"'Race' is not something certain bodies possess," writes Deborah Thomas.

> Race, here, is not an "elective identity marker" but a historical, structured, and relational experience. This experience, of course, is grounded in local landscapes of power and aspiration, themselves structured by the specific colonial histories that imbue these land-scapes with significance.[8]

Our role here isn't to interpret identity—to say what Jakes is or what anyone is, a condition some think is the purview of a nation, others the purview of a cultural community, yet others the dominion of science and biology, and still others the domain of our relations with a divinity or our ancestors.[9] And it is not ours to say what and

7. Under U.S. law, *Indian* is defined as any person who is a member of a federally recognized tribe, 25 U.S.C. § 479. For federal recognition as an Indian Tribe, federal law requires showing a history of recognition: "a body of Indians of the same or a similar race, united in a community under one leadership or government, and inhabiting a particular though sometimes ill-defined territory." *Montoya v. United States*. These elements of ethnicity, territoriality, continuity, and leadership (Canby, *Nutshell*) define the contours of Tribal Nationhood under federal law, requiring a fictitious racial purity, centralized authority, and geographic stability that white supremacy prioritizes for its own citizens and works tirelessly to make impossible for anyone else—american democracy is by definition exclusive and singular.

8. Thomas, *Political Life*, 42.

9. Roberts, *Fatal Invention*; Zuberi, *Thicker than Blood*; TallBear, "DNA Politics."

who is Indigenous and not—that would be to take up Trust logics. We can identify what we understand as some of the limits: race and property no more make or negate Indigeneity than do firstness and diaspora. Removals, migrations, and movements—forced and chosen and in between—should not serve to vacate people of their relationships to place.[10] And as we've said before, ways of relationships to place, to its life, are central to our thinking: "what the land *as a system of reciprocal relations and obligations* can teach us about living our lives in relation to one another and the natural world in nondominating and nonexploitative terms."[11] But this is also not a rubric. To be clear, we're not offering Venn diagrams of race and Indigeneity or consenting to any new, progressive colonial mathematics of being. Rather, here we consider the broadly complex vectors of refusal, relation, and self-determination. Moreover, we are considering what Jakes' particular praxis reveals about possibility in the context of Trust. In the Cupid Shuffle appears an invocation that says Indigenous does not have to be boundaried and also does not have to be all things and so nothing. Indigenous refuses conquest colonization and refuses historic purity forged through historic and historical lies.

Jakes, Black Squanto—not simply phenotypically, archivally Black but culturally, actively, politically, historically, presently Black—commands consideration and authors new histories. Jakes' identification is anti-imperial practice. In it, Jakes invokes Squanto in name and Fanon in practice: "what Fanon alerts us to is how the act of *disciplining of thought* (the process of habitually delimiting what we know about blackness according to colonial perimeters) stabilizes race and perpetuates anti-blackness."[12] And the *process of habitually delimiting what we know* about Indigeneity through conquest parameters achieves anti-Indigeneity. And those two are interknit through multiple threads, some of which are the same thread.

10. Byrd, *Transit*.
11. Coulthard, *Red Skin*, 13, italics original.
12. McKittrick, *Demonic Grounds*, 5.

Those disciplined thought perimeters and parameters regularly iterate as deterministic control—over myths of purity and their instantiating materialities. Jakes' self-determined habitation of identity, his wholeness-as-plurality, is an affront to that puritanical and ethnonationalist control. Across his refusals, he defies fragmented, fractionalized notions of race and descent, of what it means to be a person and so free.

What is you really? is the anemic lifeblood of trusteeship, conquest life-support nursed along by coerced and collusive transfusions: quantums and one-drops and enrollments and recognitions[13] and missing and murder. Purity and its antitheses—dilution, fractionalization, contamination—are imperial fictions that have long been embedded in the legal structures of the United States and the concomitant ideas of peoples. Less than whole. Reduced to a hand. Dismembered. These disciplining forces of thought pump the very heart of Trust and are parts of its desperate invention. They write the DNA of unfreedom. But dilutions and fractions are diasporic conditions, and diaspora is not simply a condition of having been scattered but rather one of possibility, generativity, invention, and freedom.[14]

Lifeblood—tainted, fractional—is in fact water, and whole. "Water is about the movement and form of when and how and with whom we know, and not merely what we claim or make claims on."[15] Stalked by the claim-staking interrogative *What is you really?* Jakes undresses the entrapping, regulatory performativity of it all, laying bare a possibility through active radical refusal: joy. In this refusal, Jakes unfurls frail plantation cartographies that link Plimoth to the Mississippi Delta to the hills of Rome, thanksgivings to slave codes to papal bulls, 1492 to 1619 to 1865 to 1924 to 1954, and Squanto to Luther Standing Bear to Jakes to the Sabines.

13. Owens, "As If"; Shanley, "Love and Read"; Vizenor, *Manifest Manners*.

14. Hall, "Cultural Identity"; Gilroy, *Black Atlantic*; McKittrick, "Who Do You Talk To"; Brand, *In Another Place*; Hartman, *Lose Your Mother*.

15. Barker, "Confluence," 6.

The law, race, *progressive* conquest time, rape, numbers, and the plantation and reservation draw us back to our apogee questions of what it means to be self-determined, to be human, in the school–prison trust. What it means to consider refusal, humor, music, dance, laughter—*the affective dimensions of experience.* We have suggested that self-determination is an enactment of sovereignty, and perhaps an umbrella for *what sovereignty feels like.* Jakes' self-determination here is a convergence and a disruption of the determined alignment of individuals, communities, nations, and race. He mobilizes identity not as a coagulated claim to disciplined purities but rather as a relational practice of difference.

As Stuart Hall writes, identity occurs in discursive relationship—through an always-ongoing, uneven process of identification—is never whole, and is unsettled in character:

> Identities are never unified and . . . increasingly fragmented and fractured; never singular but multiply constructed across different, often intersecting and antagonistic discourses, practices and positions. . . . We need to understand them as produced in specific historical and institutional sites. . . . Moreover, they emerge within the play of specific modalities of power, and thus are more the product of the marking of difference and exclusion, than they are the sign of an identical, naturally constituted unity. . . . Above all . . . identities are constructed through, not outside, difference.[16]

Complex processes of identification[17] and disidentification[18] have offered us dynamic anticolonial understandings and possibilities,[19]

16. Hall, "Who Needs 'Identity,'" 17.

17. Mercer, *Travel and See*; Hall, "Who Needs 'Identity.'" "Identification is, then, a process of articulation, a suturing, an overdetermination or a lack, but never a proper fit, a totality." Hall, 17.

18. Muñoz, *Disidentifications.* "The process of disidentification scrambles and reconstructs the encoded message of a cultural text in a fashion that both exposes the encoded message's universalizing and exclusionary machinations and recircuits its workings to account for, include, and empower minority identities and identifications" (31).

19. Many cultural studies scholars have examined the concept of hybridity. Muñoz, for example, writes, "*Hybrid* catches the fragmentary

particularly as we think about the *historical and institutional sites* of the school–prison trust. At the crux of these processes is imperialism.

In *Culture and Imperialism*, Edward Said writes, "New alignments made across borders, types, nations and essences . . . now provoke and challenge the fundamentally static notion of *identity* that has been the core of cultural thought during the era of imperialism."[20] We take seriously the identity-based disciplining of thought that entrenches conquest power and stalls insurgent freedom. As Said writes, identity was imperialism's "worst and most paradoxical gift."[21]

Its worst and most paradoxical gift is also, instructively, one of imperialism's vulnerabilities. In *Forgeries of Memory and Meaning*, Robinson connects imperialism's identity forces to racial regime decay:

> With respect to the social terrain, the degeneration of racial regimes occurs with some frequency for two reasons. First, apparent difference in identity is an attempt to mask shared identities. . . . A second source of regime entropy ensues from the fact that because the regimes are cultural artifices, which catalogue only fragments of the real, they inevitably generate fugitive, unaccounted-for elements of reality.[22]

As he wrote in *Black Movements*, it was indeed the grand lie of white racial solidarity (a solidarity imagined to trump class and all other powered dimensions of societal life but which shatters at the moment it encounters those dimensions), and ongoing white collusion with it, that masked shared identities around other domains of human life.[23]

---

subject formation of people whose identities traverse different race, sexuality, and gender identifications" (31).

20. Said, *Culture and Imperialism*, 336.
21. Said.
22. Robinson, *Forgeries*, xiii.
23. Robinson, *Black Movements*.

This grand lie is as evident in the continuous making of the school–prison trust as anywhere, and it is as tied in that Trust context to the imperialist union of identity and nation expressed in *national identity* as necessary for upholding supremacist destinies. In his invocations and performances of identity as dis/identification, we understand Jakes' joyful, angry, incisive refusals as processes of anti-imperialism, movements against the identity–nation–destiny circuitry of the governing ideas of Trust. To be self-determining, to shrug off the colonial naming mechanisms (via contamination or dilution or fractionation), to counter imperialist disciplining through identity and nation, is to point to free futures.

Futures

Prompted by Jakes' praxis of multiplicity in this imperial context, we circle back to wonder how an attention to time, race, and western monastic capitalist epistemologies might reveal brittle apertures through which free futures burst forward. Together.

Futures don't exist only in some dreamy horizon-time. They aren't solely far off or fantastical or the stuff of destinies, even though they are of those things too. Futures were also made in and by the near and very distant past. And futures are made not only by people but also by the agentive and constrained force of the cosmos and all creation. Futures are also being made now. By us, growing from the present as we actively make them. As we see it, there are multiple possible futures being made right now, and the juridical, militarized, temporal, doctrinal, gendered, terrortorial, self-determined, refusal, racialized, propertied, eschatalogical, maternalist, sovereign, and memoried dynamics of the school–prison trust provide a porthole and a portal to futures we have to grapple with now.

As Arundhati Roy entreats, "the urge for hegemony and preponderance by some will be matched with greater intensity by the longing for dignity and justice by others. Exactly what form that takes, whether it's beautiful or bloodthirsty, depends on us."[24]

24. Roy, *Public Power*, 59.

Confiscated Time, and One Futurity

"When we ask ourselves whether it's inhumane to inflict a certain technology on someone, we have to make sure it's not just the unfamiliarity that spooks us." Thus is framed the philosophical question that guides one devastating experiment in carcerality.[25]

Western philosophical thought can ask, without being instantaneously disintegrated by the horrifically impossible contradiction of moral atoms colliding, if *inflicting* something on someone can be understood as humane (to the inflictor, we assume). There's this received convention in critical circles that power doesn't get decided around a table in smoky, windowless rooms. But actually that's sometimes precisely how it gets decided. Often in the case of western philosophical thought, it is as if its philosophers sit at their pleasant, liberal, genocidal dinner table swirling Bordeaux, discerning types of humans and their therefore relative experience of humanity in the same breath as shoes or vacations or vapid politics or whatever it is they discuss.

At one such table, the hors d'oeuvres have been served and "a team of scholars [is] focused upon the ways futuristic technologies might transform punishment"—specifically, how they might make it "worse."[26] How delightful. Along with the carpaccio. The delicious rawness of it all.

And the specific topic of their deliberative attention? Time. It seems that drug or computer intercession on the mind could modify the imprisoned person's experience of time, converting hours into years, or a millennium. This is no hyperbole on our part. In an interview, philosopher Roache explained,

> If the speed-up were a factor of a million, a millennium of thinking would be accomplished in eight and a half hours. . . . Uploading the mind of a convicted criminal and running it a million times faster

25. Williams, "Prisoners Could Serve."
26. Williams.

than normal would enable the uploaded criminal to serve a 1,000 year sentence in eight-and-a-half hours. This would, obviously, be much cheaper for the taxpayer than extending criminals' lifespans to enable them to serve 1,000 years in real time.[27]

There is utility here, they might imagine, joyriding one particular western philosophical tradition. But it alone does not answer nagging ethical considerations, particularly in the empire progenitor context, where this question is being taken up (and funded).

Time, its making and unmaking, its assignation of beginnings, its geometric flattening into lines, has always been an implement of conquest. This philosophers' torture party reveals ways in which western conquest is innate to liberal western thought and inimical to any freedom. The confiscation of human time as a sustained act of conquest is warcraft. It works in cosmic and intimate scales to pillage a future.

This future-plunder is of the most barbaric sort. The proposition is simple, and in it the zenith and nadir of conquest terror meet. By speeding up time, these philosophers, these lovers of pure form, are suggesting removing the possibility for relationality. They are in fact describing a kind of solitary confinement previously unimagined—one that guts what it means to be human with a jagged paring knife. Prisons, for all their horror, are still places where people form and forge reciprocal, refusal relationships, where *disciplining of thought*—for all its architectural, psychological, panoptical industriousness—is still very much contested, resisted, negotiated. Where—for all the efforts at spirit murder[28] and its agnates—human beings can still dream self-determinedly. What these thought conquerors suggest is to *kill the dream in him* and leave a placeless, relationless carcass with only a mind to observe that total terror.

"And a man without dreams is just a meaty machine with a broken gauge."[29]

27. Williams.
28. Williams, *Alchemy*.
29. Dimaline, *Marrow Thieves*, 88.

"Movement and Form"

The fervor in the goal to make carcasses of humans mimics the western zealotry for gutting memory and the metaphysical in the social realm. Yet, humans are never simply the entrails of regimes and their massacres. Other futures are being made right now, and it is all of ours to nurture those, not simply stop the philosophers' future. Possible militancy, or refusal, or radicalism, or resistance, or resurgence, does not emerge solely from the abject condition of oppression. As Cedric Robinson argues,

> the social cauldron of Black radicalism is Western society. Western society, however, has been its location and its objective condition but not—except in a most perverse fashion—its inspiration. Black radicalism is a negation of Western civilization, but not in the direct sense of a simple dialectical negation. It is certain that the evolving tradition of Black radicalism owes its peculiar moment to the historical interdiction of African life by European agents. . . . This experience, though, was merely the condition for Black radicalism . . . but not the foundation for its nature or character. Black radicalism, consequently, cannot be understood within the particular context of its genesis.[30]

It is, as Robinson argues, the metaphysical—the greater ontological spirit not shaped in relation or reaction to westernness—that dialectically shapes Black radicalism. Likewise, Indigenous refusal finds as its *cauldron,* its *location* and *condition,* conquest colonization's ideological materialization in Trust, but Trust is not its *inspiration.* Refusal is the *negation* of the ideology of Trust, but not as an antagonism, opposite, or antithesis. Rather, refusal is of the ontological, the metaphysical, of knowledges outside and unparallel to the narrow epistemes of conquest.

The spirit of radical imagination that is the ontological throughline of self-determination is engendered everywhere, in part through common cause. Decolonization or anticolonization and

30. Robinson, *Black Marxism,* 72–73.

abolition share such common purposes or cause and, in the case of the school–prison trust, suggest to us that we must at least be curious about the legal, doctrinal codifications that are the very real custom and command contexts of Trust. Even if fleeting or itinerant, are there possibilities or necessities toward freedom in the law?

This brief foray of ours takes place within what we hope is the long overdue disintegration of meliorism and its henchmen—and that tradition's colossal structure: conquest capitalism's democracy. James Boggs describes democracy as a global phenomenon of power that, at its best, allows occasional negotiation but preempts any "revolution" particularly through its reliance on majority rule.[31] Along with numerous other scholars, Boggs situates it as endemic to capitalism and as a feature necessary to continued exploitation of labor and resources. Other scholars have considered its relationship to colonialism across numerous material, ideological vectors.[32]

As we witness and participate in *the disintegration,* we abide the complex insistence that freedom efforts must of course live in the tension of the contemporary world, and therefore painstakingly refuse to signify and secure the state's authority to determine futures while simultaneously ministering structurally with the full resources available with, to, and for those people repressed and in captivity now. For the school–prison trust, then, we see tentative possibilities for sovereign futures, beyond Trust.

Notably, Dorothy Roberts observes that in the *longue durée* of Black abolitionism in the United States, incarcerated abolitionists and their legal advocates have used the constitution to "articulate and present the demands of people subjected to carceral punishment . . . even when they anticipate failure."[33] But as Joy James writes, "neither advocacy abolitionism nor state abolitionism can control or create freedom." Indeed, at their best, they can only con-

---

31. Boggs, *Racism.*

32. Brayboy, "Tribal Critical Race Theory"; Grande, "American Indian Geographies"; Denetdale, "Chairmen"; Piatote, *Domestic Subjects.*

33. Roberts, "Abolition Constitutionalism," 113.

fer "emancipation." "Emancipation is *given* by the dominant, it being a legal, contractual, and social agreement. Freedom is *taken* and created."[34] What, we wonder, might this mean for Trust, when its abolition is currently correspondent with termination—of Nations and individuals? What does this mean in the context of the school–prison trust as warcraft?

As Dylan Rodríguez lays out in *Forced Passages,* the U.S. prison regime is domestic war.[35] The school–prison trust operates at the fiery collision point of domestic and conquest wars and their implements: domestic and international doctrine, law, and treaties; domestic and international self-determination and refusal; domestic and international ideologies and epistemologies. And that collision point is mapped onto global terrains of power. Moreover, it is mapped onto compounding complexities: schools have indeed been self-determinedly made and mobilized as sites for freedom work, whereas, while such work has been undertaken within prisons, prisons have never been made for freedom futures. Because the school–prison trust moves through peoples—and almost never in neat, analytic, structural separation, as it did in the boarding and residential school eras—and because multiplicity moves in and through peoples, free futures must be deeply overlapping and co-alitional even as they maintain richly distinct understandings, and they must contend with the complex collisional nature of sites and systems of unfreedom.

The futures without the warfare of the school–prison trust that might burst forth from the right-now necessarily come in some part from struggling with the conquest nation's legal regime. They also come from collective, careful pedagogical and other knowledge praxes. They come from a radical resurgence of knowing together.

Dian Million, in her gift of an essay entitled "There Is a River in Me: Theory from Life" invites and commands us to the right-now:

---

34. James, introduction to *New Abolitionists,* xxii.
35. Rodriguez, *Forced Passages.*

So, what do we know that we might act from? We are living in a time when the most vulnerable die (this includes many, many life-forms), a worldwide experience that affects our vital relations with life itself. There is a struggle against the capitalization, the commoditization of life even as it is happening. . . . Our collective history-filled space here is not a void . . . the space is filled with the emotional resonance of our actions in this place.[36]

Resonant Futurities

Langston Hughes understands that the world is marked on its own terms, by earth, life, and water:

I've known rivers:
I've known rivers ancient as the world and older than the
    flow of human blood in human veins.[37]

Conquest cartographers marked the world on parchment—most often the untreated skins of animals ransacked for the properties of their carcasses, properties of susceptibility to the recording of plunder and all its claims. As they marked the former home of the creature with their most permanent ink, they made heaviest the lines that were meant to reveal the shape of land. Almost as if natural and eternal borders encased place.

But we know that heavy line to be, in actuality, a place among the most volatile, most pliable, most definitively impermanent.[38] Where the shore and the ocean meet is abundantly, exuberantly relational. No two tides mark the same shadow as they recede. No sand or pebble stays locked in place. No droplets of water crash together or swirl in the same way twice. Yet an entire teeming world lives there—between low and high tide; between storm and calm;

---

36. Million, "River in Me," 32.
37. Excerpt from Hughes, "The Negro Speaks of Rivers."
38. Brayboy, "Tidemarks"; Green, "What's in a Tidemark."

ice and currents—reminding us that bounded permanence, too, is a controlling invention of conquest.

There are other futures, unbounded. The future is an idea/idea is the future. In "Some Like Indians Endure," Paula Gunn Allen writes,

> the idea which
> once you have it
> you can't be taken
> for somebody else . . .[39]

The idea is a resonant link. We've watched the idea of memory as self-determined, relationally refusing. We've seen the idea of time as partner and slipstream. We've heard the idea of names and watched their puff emerge as powerful actors. *The idea* is a willing willful movement from and toward unpredictable and yet practiced possibility—of worlds outside conquest, of dimensions unimaginable in empire cartographies and calendars, of names we'll remember when we hear them for the first time—where we will find out what is there, and where we know one thing for certain: abiding, deep connection will be our guide.

Life Is Precious

Life is precious[40] not because or when it's exceptional—exceptionally good or exceptionally bad. Most of us most of the time are just moving through or being in the simple, mundane of our hours and days. Sometimes we're funny, and sometimes we're jerks, and sometimes for a minute we're pretty insightful.

In this hour of this day, Desmond was working blandly on a multiple-choice handout. He was a serious, though not terribly thoughtful, young person. I often wondered if he was just fundamentally tired. At any rate, he had asked me to help him out, even

39. Allen, "Some Like Indians Endure," 9–13.
40. Gilmore, "Is Prison Necessary?"

though there was nothing to help with. He was smart. This was inane busy work. So I sat with him on the long side of the work table to keep him company, and we both pretended I was helping.

Across the table, Jakes drew insect-headed, semi-human-bodied anime-like figures on his handout. They jumped around the questions, stretched into the margins, dallied between choices. I strained my eyes to read their speech bubbles—upside down and in dull, prison-issued number 2 pencil.

The time moved on this way, Desmond and I pretending our roles, Jakes lost in another universe, me glancing over regularly in admiration and curiosity. There was no particular beginning or end. Or middle.

But there were moments, of all sorts. This one was Jakes and our teeth.

Looking at a particularly odd multiple-choice question on Desmond's handout, I apparently enlisted my facial expression in my thinking. Occasionally in life, I squinch up my brow, press my tongue against the back of my top teeth, and mutter something to the effect of "huh." In this expression, my front two teeth show in full.

"Hey!" Jakes must have taken a pause from his worksheet bugworld-making and seen me. "Hey! Sabina!"

"Yeah?" I looked up. He was pointing up at his front teeth.

"Check it out. See? We got the same cracked tooth." He pressed his pointer finger against the small cutout in his upper right tooth.

I prefer "chipped" to "cracked," I thought, but went along with it. "I was wondering if you were gonna notice that," I smiled.

"Dude," Jakes whisper-yelled to Desmond as the teacher glanced over in a halfhearted threat. "Dude, check it out. We got matching tooth cracks."

Desmond looked at the two of us, revealing our chipped teeth for him. He nodded. "Yeah, man."

"How you get yours?" Jakes asked, gesturing at my face with his chin. Avoiding the teacher's interest, Desmond pointed to something on his handout, and I looked down.

"Beat the crap out of someone," I said, nonchalant, not looking up.

It was a little bit smart-ass teasing, a little bit making fun of myself. (I think, actually, I got it opening a lid to something. Unexciting and probably embarrassing, if I thought too much about it.)

"What about you?" I followed casually.

"*Actually* beat the crap out of someone." I could hear the priceless satisfaction in his deft, quick retort.

"Well, yours is pretty," I said to Jakes, looking up.

"Yeah?" Suddenly he was sweetness and yearning.

"Yeah," I confirmed.

"Yeah, man," said Desmond.

Desmond and I returned to pretending. Jakes went back to his other-universe doodles. His multiple-choice, slipstream handout a portal to a teeming world of insect-humans, with a cracked-tooth leader named Jakes.

Acknowledgments

We wrote this book across six states, through five jobs, in a pandemic, from basements, offices, airplanes, airbnbs, minivans, and lake homes, in celebrations and sadnesses and all the in-between. It's hard to say where it started, because it has many origins. But the old adage that "it takes a village" remains true with this collective effort. So, we offer some shared thanks here.

There are a number of individuals we want to collectively acknowledge. Patty Ferguson-Bohnee, executive director of the Indian Legal Program at Arizona State University, and Bryan invited Sabina to a town hall called "School-to-Prison Pipeline in Indian Country: Mapping Out Solutions," hosted by the Indian Legal Program. It was at this conference that Sabina presented the initial iteration of what would later become this book: "'A More Sophisticated Technique': Child Trust." In its earliest stages, Nicholas Bustamante was part of important conversations. Andrea Underwood, in the Center for Indian Education at ASU, provided administrative assistance with travel and other financial engagements. Lindsey Hawker, Bryan's colleague at ASU, scheduled our meetings and helped keep us organized. Thank you to Tufts University and the University of Washington for hosting our in-person writings—when in-person was still a thing. We are grateful to several people and groups who read drafts of the book and whose insights and engagements made it infinitely stronger: Damien Sojoyner; Kirsten Edwards; Stacey Lee;

Jennifer Johnson; Kyle Halle-Erby; Melissa Colón; Chris Wright; the Prisons, Schools, and Abolition Freedom Seminar members; Adrienne Keene; Kailah Carden; and the Revere High School Study Group, to name a few. At the invitation of Drs. Amanda Tachine and Eve Ewing, we shared portions of the book at their summer 2021 conference, "Cultivating Black and Native Futures in Education," and received generous feedback. We are grateful to Tanaya Winder, an enrolled member of the Duckwater Shoshone Tribe, for her generosity in allowing us to use excerpts of her poem "We Were Stolen." The poem appears in her book *Why Storms Are Named After People and Bullets Remain Nameless.* Thank you, Tanaya. We're grateful for early conversations with Pieter Martin at the University of Minnesota Press. Later, we worked with Eric Lundgren and Leah Pennywark in the Forerunner series. Their feedback and guidance, along with those of the reviewer, were crucial to the completion of this book. Christy McGuire, a doctoral student at the University of Pittsburgh, helped with early book formatting. And the copy editing team at the University of Minnesota Press was of tremendous support. Finally, we had to cut more than half our footnotes, so we thank all those scholars whose influences are in this book but whose names are not.

JEREMIAH: First and foremost, I thank Bryan McKinley Jones Brayboy and Sabina Vaught, not just for this collaborative project of writing a book, but for mentoring me and putting me in position to actually come to the text and write and think in novel and different ways. It is not often that you get to meet your heroes and even rarer when they turn out to be inviting collaborators and co-conspirators who generate knowledge to share and encourage those who are lucky enough to enter their orbit. A thousand thank-yous is not enough for their mentorship and support in this process. For drafting this piece, a tremendous thank-you to Nicholas Bustamante, who started on the journey writing about the school-to-prison pipeline with me, about which we were then able to present our data and start talking with Sabina. A few special thank-yous to those who have supported this writing but whom I would feel remiss not to note personally: thank you to the Center for Indian Education, particularly Bryan Brayboy, Lindsay Hawker, and Andrea Underwood, for providing financial, practical, and technical support in my travels to write and collaborate with Sabina at Tufts University and the University of Washington; thank you to the Indian Legal Program (ILP) at Arizona State University, especially Kate Rosier, Patty Ferguson-Bohnee, Greg Hill, and Ann Marie Bledsoe Downes, for providing me a space to learn as a law student, come into community, join in conversations on Indian law in novel and complex ways, and learn from the many scholars who inspired and continue to inspire my writings. Particular thanks to Rebecca Tsosie, Robert Clinton, and Robert Miller for training me in "Federal Indian Law" and "Tribal Law and Government" to give me the depth and breadth of understanding to contribute to the conversation on trusteeship in an informed and meaningful way. Finally, thank you to my favorite person, Keeonna Harris, for listening to my ramblings about trusteeship and supporting me through hours of Zoom calls. Most important, thank you to Keeonna, Zion, Xi, and Olajide every day, for reminding me of the importance of joy.

BRYAN: I am grateful to both Sabina and Jeremiah for sharing this journey with me. Sabina's ability to take our ideas, craft them into a voice that reflected our collective vision, and do so quickly is wondrous. Sabina is one of the best writers I know; seeing her process words was like watching a gifted musician play. Jeremiah's ability to take complex ideas, condense them into a tasty word roux, and serve them to us graciously (and humbly!) was a lovely gift. Jeremiah and Sabina are the very best of brilliance, humility, and good humor wrapped together. In the midst of our Friday afternoon conversations and writings, I sometimes wondered, "What am I doing here, sandwiched between two brilliant minds and amazing humans?" I'm lucky. And grateful. Lindsey Hawker manages me with grace and kindness, making it possible for me to find time for this endeavor of love. And, finally, my family (Doris Warriner, Quanah and Ely Brayboy) remain a constant source of love and awe. Our sons—Indigenous young men around the same age as Jakes when Sabina worked with him—are a reason and inspiration for my work.

SABINA: To the two most extraordinary coauthors a person could have, thank you. Both of you are bring-you-to-your-knees brilliant. Funny as hell. Kind. But descriptors won't capture how I experienced the gifts you all give to me and the world. After a year and a half of Friday Zooms, pink-green-blue Google Docs, "ink it!" exclamations, too many footnotes, and never enough time, I'm profoundly and forever changed by you. Bryan and Jeremiah, I love you guys. To so many colleagues, students, teachers, and friends along the way, I'm grateful for your intellectual companionship. A special shout out to Heather Shotton and the members of the Rematriation dream course for the profound space we made and shared; it inspired me. To the radical student collective for the invigorating intellectual hours over savory vegan waffles, crispy brussels sprouts, and beans and rice. And to Kirsten Edwards and the Women and Girls Collective for coming together through differences, imposed and felt, for beautiful common cause. Kathy Woodward and the Simpson Center for the Humanities at the University of Washington awarded me the scholarly residency that afforded time and space to undertake contributions to this project. Joanna and Brenda (Broanna, affectionately), thank you for the early-pandemic rescue and the shared space that was a home to the first draft of this book. Jakes, I hope this book thanks you a little bit. You deserve the world. My mom. I remember my first visit to my mom's home after my last book was published. After the six-hour flight, the late-night, rainy drive in the Lyft to the top of her driveway, and the dragging of my way-too-heavy suitcase full of gifts down that gravel stretch, I finally got to her door. She was ill then. Sitting on her couch, she beamed at me as I walked in the house. She got up gingerly, moving toward me for a long-anticipated hug. On the little table next to her spot on the couch, I saw my book prominently displayed, spine out, just *under* Christina Sharpe's *In the Wake* (which I had given her). I burst into laughter and hugged her tight in gratitude. I miss so much all the ways you pushed me, Mom. I wonder now which book she would place on top of this one, even as she would tell Bryan and Jeremiah that this book is the best she's ever read. My biggest champions and smartest critics, Cecilia, Carmen, and Satya. They made me countless smoothies, kept me sharp even when I didn't want to be, and read, listened to, and talked through every draft, starting from that talk I gave in 2017. But the best thing they did was to decide, over and over, despite and because of it all, to live beautiful lives. I love you girls.

Bibliography

Alfred, T. "Sovereignty." In *Sovereignty Matters*, edited by Joanne Barker, 33–50. Lincoln: University of Nebraska Press, 2005.

Allen, Paula G. "Some Like Indians Endure." In *Living the Spirit: A Gay American Indian Anthology*, edited by Will Roscoe, 9–13. New York: St. Martin's Press, 1988.

Anderson, Kim, Maria Campbell, and Christi Belcourt. *Keetsahnak: Our Missing and Murdered Indigenous Sisters*. Edmonton: University of Alberta Press, 2018.

AP News. "The Latest: South African Pleads Not Guilty in Alaska Death." October 21, 2019. https://apnews.com/article/7f7cc0cfeab843239c4e602806598aee.

Baldwin, James. *The Fire Next Time*. New York: Dial Press, 1963.

Baldwin, James, Emile Capouya, Lorraine Hansberry, Nat Hentoff, Langston Hughes, and Alfred Kazin. "The Negro in American Culture." *CrossCurrents* 11, no. 3 (1961): 205–24.

Balibar, Étienne. "The Nation Form: History and Ideology." *Review (Fernand Braudel Center)* 13, no. 3 (1990): 329–61.

Barker, Joanne. "Confluence: Water as an Analytic of Indigenous Feminisms." *American Indian Culture and Research Journal* 43, no. 3 (2019): 1–40. https://doi.org/10.17953/aicrj.43.3.barker.

Barker, Joanne, ed. *Sovereignty Matters*. Lincoln: University of Nebraska Press, 2005.

Basso, Keith H. *Wisdom Sits in Places: Landscape and Language among the Western Apache*. Albuquerque: University of New Mexico Press, 1996.

Belcourt, Billy-Ray. *This Wound Is a World*. Minneapolis: University of Minnesota Press, 2019.

Bendery, Jennifer. "Congress Finally Passes Bill to Address Missing and Murdered Indigenous Women. Native American Women Are Disappearing and Being Killed: Savanna's Act Will Help Bring Them Some Justice." *Huffington Post*, September 21, 2020. https://www

.huffpost.com/entry/missing-murdered-indigenous-women-congress
-savannas-act-murkowski_n_5f690b2bc5b63b8afd80ff43.

Blu, Karen. "'Where Do You Stay At?': Homeplace and Community among
the Lumbee." In *Sense of Place*, edited by Steven Feld and Keith H.
Basso, 197–227. Santa.Fe, N.M.: School of American Research Press,
1996.

Boggs, J. *Racism and the Class Struggle: Further Pages from a Black
Worker's Notebook*. New York: Monthly Review Press, 1970.

Brand, Dionne. *In Another Place, Not Here*. New York: Grove Press, 2000.

Brayboy, Bryan M. J. "Tidemarks and Legacies: Building on the Past and
Moving to the Future." *Anthropology and Education Quarterly* 44, no. 1
(2013): 1–10. https://doi.org/10.1111/aeq.12001.

Brayboy, Bryan M. J. "Toward a Tribal Critical Race Theory in
Education." *Urban Review* 37, no. 5 (2005): 425–46. https://doi
.org/10.1007/s11256-005-0018-y.

Brayboy, Bryan M. J., and Jeremiah Chin. "On the Development
of Terrortory." *Contexts* 19, no. 3 (2020): 22–27. https://doi.
org/10.1177/1536504220950397.

Brown, Wendy A. "Finding the Man in the State." *Feminist Studies* 18, no. 1
(1992): 7. https://doi.org/10.2307/3178212.

Byrd, Jodi A. *The Transit of Empire: Indigenous Critiques of Colonialism*.
Minneapolis: University of Minnesota Press, 2011.

Canby, William C., Jr. *American Indian Law in a Nutshell*. 6th ed. St. Paul,
Minn.: West Academic, 2015.

Carby, Hazel V. *Reconstructing Womanhood: The Emergence of the Afro-
American Woman Novelist*. New York: Oxford University Press, 1989.

Carrier Sekani Family Services. "Highway of Tears." http://www
.highwayoftears.org/.

Ceci, Lynn. "Squanto and the Pilgrims: On Planting Corn 'in the Manner
of the Indians.'" In *The Invented Indian: Cultural Fictions and
Government Policies*, edited by James A. Clifton, 71–90. New York:
Routledge, 2017.

Cherokee Nation v. Georgia, 30 U.S. (5 Pet.) 1 (1831).

Child, Brenda J. *Boarding School Seasons: American Indian Families, 1900–
1940*. Lincoln: University of Nebraska Press, 2012.

Coalition to Stop Violence against Native Women. "MMIW." https://www
.csvanw.org/mmiw/.

Coffey, Wallace, and Rebecca Tsosie. "Rethinking the Tribal Sovereignty
Doctrine." *Stanford Law and Policy Review* 12, no. 2 (2001): 191–221.

Cohen, Felix. "Transcendental Nonsense and the Functional Approach."
Columbia Law Review 35, no. 6 (1935): 814–17. https://doi
.org/10.2307/1116300.

Coulthard, Glen S. *Red Skin, White Masks: Rejecting the Colonial Politics of
Recognition*. Minneapolis: University of Minnesota Press, 2014.

Davis, Angela Y. *Are Prisons Obsolete?* New York: Seven Stories Press, 2003.

Deal, Gregg. "The Last American Indian on Earth." April 27, 2016. http:// greggdeal.com/The-Last-American-Indian-On-Earth-1.

Deer, Sarah. *The Beginning and End of Rape: Confronting Sexual Violence in Native America.* Minneapolis: University of Minnesota Press, 2015.

Deloria, Philip J. *Playing Indian.* New Haven, Conn.: Yale University Press, 1998.

Deloria, Vine, Jr. *Behind the Trail of Broken Treaties: An Indian Declaration of Independence.* 3rd ed. Austin: University of Texas Press, 1990.

Deloria, Vine, Jr. *Custer Died for Your Sins: An Indian Manifesto.* Norman: University of Oklahoma Press, 1988.

Deloria, Vine, Jr. *We Talk, You Listen: New Tribes, New Turf.* Lincoln: University of Nebraska Press, 1970.

Deloria, Vine, Jr. and Daniel R. Wildcat. *Power and Place: Indian Education in America.* Golden, Colo.: Fulcrum Resources, 2001.

Denetdale, Jennifer. "Chairmen, Presidents, and Princesses: The Navajo Nation, Gender, and the Politics of Tradition." *Wíčazo Ša Review* 21, no. 1 (2006): 9–28. https://doi.org/10.1353/wic.2006.0004.

Diaz, Natalie. *Postcolonial Love Poem.* Minneapolis, Minn.: Graywolf Press, 2020.

Dimaline, Cherie. *The Marrow Thieves.* Toronto, Ont.: Cormorant Books, 2017.

Erdrich, Louise. *The Antelope Wife.* New York: Harper Perennial, 1998.

Erdrich, Louise. *Four Souls.* New York: Harper Perennial, 2004.

Erdrich, Louise. *The Last Report on the Miracles at Little No Horse.* New York: Harper Perennial, 2001.

Erdrich, Louise. *The Night Watchman.* New York: Harper Perennial, 2020.

Fanon, Frantz. *Black Skin, White Masks.* New York: Grove Press, 1952.

Fletcher, Matthew L. M., and Wenona T. Singel. "Indian Children and the Federal–Tribal Trust Relationship." *Nebraska Law Review* 95, no. 4 (2017): 885–964.

Furlow, Bryant. "A Hospital's Secret Coronavirus Policy Separated Native American Mothers from Their Newborns." *ProPublica,* June 13, 2020. https://www.propublica.org/article/a-hospitals-secret-coronavirus -policy-separated-native-american-mothers-from-their-newborns.

Gilmore, Ruth W. *Golden Gulag: Prisons, Surplus, Crisis, and Opposition in Globalizing California.* Berkeley: University of California Press, 2007.

Gilmore, Ruth W. "Is Prison Necessary?" *New York Times,* April 17, 2019. https://www.nytimes.com/2019/04/17/magazine/prison-abolition -ruth-wilson-gilmore.html.

Gilpin, Lyndsey. "Native American Women Still Have the Highest Rates of Rape and Assault." *High Country News,* June 7, 2016. https://www.hcn .org/articles/tribal-affairs-why-native-american-women-still-have -the-highest-rates-of-rape-and-assault.

Gilroy, Paul. *The Black Atlantic: Modernity and Double-Consciousness.* Cambridge, Mass.: Harvard University Press, 1995.

Goeman, Mishuana R. *Mark My Words: Native Women Mapping Our Nations.* Minneapolis: University of Minnesota Press, 2013.

Goeman, Mishuana R. "Notes toward a Native Feminism's Spatial Practice." *Wíčazo Ša Review* 24, no. 2 (2009): 169–87. https://doi .org/10.1353/wic.0.0040.

Goeman, Mishuana R. "Ongoing Storms and Struggles: Gendered Violence and Resource Exploitation." In *Critically Sovereign: Indigenous Gender, Sexuality, and Feminist Studies,* edited by Joanne Barker, 99–126. Durham, N.C.: Duke University Press, 2017.

Goldberg, Carole E. "Overextended Borrowing: Tribal Peacemaking Applied in Non-Indian Disputes." *Washington Law Review* 72, no. 4 (1997): 1003–20.

Goodyear-Kaʻōpua, Noelani. "Indigenous Oceanic Futures: Challenging Settler Colonialisms and Militarization." In *Indigenous and Decolonizing Studies in Education: Mapping the Long View,* edited by Linda T. Smith, Eve Tuck, and K. Wayne Yang, 82–102. New York: Routledge, 2018.

Goodyear-Kaʻōpua, Noelani. *The Seeds We Planted: Portraits of a Native Hawaiian Charter School.* Minneapolis: University of Minnesota Press, 2013.

Grande, Sandy. "American Indian Geographies of Identity and Power: At the Crossroads of Indígena and Mestizaje." *Harvard Educational Review* 70, no. 4 (2000): 467–99. https://doi.org/10.17763 /haer.70.4.47717110136rvt53.

Grande, Sandy, and Teresa L. McCarty. "Indigenous Elsewheres: Refusal and Re-membering in Education Research, Policy, and Praxis." *International Journal of Qualitative Studies in Education* 31, no. 3 (2018): 165–67. https://doi.org/10.1080/09518398.2017.1401144.

Green, Sarah. "What's in a Tidemark." *Anthropology News* 52, no. 2 (2011): 15. https://doi.org/10.1111/j.1556-3502.2011.52215.x.

Hall, Stuart. "Cultural Identity and Diaspora." In *Identity: Community, Culture, Difference,* edited by Jonathan Rutherford, 222–37. London: Lawrence and Wishart, 1990.

Hall, Stuart. "Who Needs 'Identity'?" In *Identity: A Reader,* edited by Paul Du Gay, Jessica Evans, and Peter Redman, 15–30. London: Sage, 2000.

Harjo, Joy. *Conflict Resolution for Holy Beings: Poems.* New York: W. W. Norton, 2015.

Harjo, Laura. *Spiral to the Stars: Mvskoke Tools of Futurity.* Tucson: University of Arizona Press, 2019.

Harney, Fred, and Stefano Moten. *The Undercommons: Fugitive Planning and Black Study.* New York: Autonomedia, 2013.

Harris, Cheryl. "Whiteness as Property." *Harvard Law Review* 106, no. 8 (1993): 1709–91. https://doi.org/10.2307/1341787.

Hartman, Saidiya V. *Lose Your Mother: A Journey along the Atlantic Slave Route*. New York: Farrar, Straus, and Giroux, 2007.

Hu, Jane C. "One Woman Took a Stand against Tribal Disenrollment and Paid for It." *High Country News,* February 1, 2020. https://www.hcn.org/issues/52.2/indigenous-affairs-one-woman-took-a-stand-against-tribal-disenrollment-and-paid-for-it-nooksack.

Hughes, Langston. "The Negro Speaks of Rivers." *The Crisis,* November 1970, 366.

Jacobs, M. D. *White Mother to a Dark Race: Settler Colonialism, Maternalism, and the Removal of Indigenous Children in the American West and Australia, 1880–1940*. Lincoln: University of Nebraska Press, 2009.

James, Joy, ed. Introduction to *The New Abolitionists: (Neo)Slave Narratives and Contemporary Prison Writings*. Albany: SUNY Press, 2005.

James, Joy. *Resisting State Violence: Radicalism, Gender, and Race in US Culture*. Minneapolis: University of Minnesota Press, 1996.

James, Joy. *Warfare in the American Homeland: Policing and Prison in a Penal Democracy*. Durham, N.C.: Duke University Press, 2007.

Johnson v. M'Intosh, 21 U.S. (8 Wheat.) 543 (1823).

Kelley, Robin D. G. *Freedom Dreams: The Black Radical Imagination*. Boston: Beacon Press, 2002.

Khubchandani, Kareem. *Ishtyle: Accenting Gay Indian Nightlife*. Ann Arbor: University of Michigan Press, 2020.

Klein, Jessica. "They Survived Abuse—Now They Can't Safely Vote." October 28, 2020. https://indiancountrytoday.com/news/they-survived-abuse-now-they-cant-safely-vote.

Lavell-Harvard, D. Memee, and Jennifer Brant, eds. *Forever Loved: Exposing the Hidden Crisis of Missing and Murdered Indigenous Women and Girls in Canada*. Bradford, Ont.: Demeter Press, 2016.

Lomawaima, K. Tsianina. *They Called It Prairie Light: The Story of Chilocco Indian School*. Lincoln: University of Nebraska Press, 1995.

Lomawaima, K. Tsianina, and Teresa L. McCarty. *"To Remain an Indian": Lessons in Democracy from a Century of Native American Education*. New York: Teachers College Press, 2006.

Lorde, Audre. *Sister Outsider: Essays and Speeches*. Berkeley, Calif.: Ten Speed Press, 1984.

Lyons, Scott. "Rhetorical Sovereignty: What Do American Indians Want from Writing?" *College Composition and Communication* 51, no. 3 (2000): 447–68. https://doi.org/doi:10.2307/358744.

Major Crimes Act. 18 U.S.C. § 1153 (1885).

McClintock, Anne. "The Angel of Progress: Pitfalls of the Term 'Post-Colonialism.'" *Social Text,* no. 31/32 (1992): 84–98. https://doi.org/10.2307/466219.

McKittrick, Katherine. *Demonic Grounds: Black Women and the Cartographies of Struggle*. Minneapolis: University of Minnesota Press, 2006.

McKittrick, Katherine. "'Who Do You Talk to, When a Body's in Trouble?': M. Nourbese Philip's (Un)silencing of Black Bodies in the Diaspora." *Social and Cultural Geography* 1, no. 2 (2010): 223–36. https://doi.org/10.1080/14649360020010220.

Mercer, Kobena. *Travel and See: Black Diaspora Art Practices since the 1980s*. Durham, N.C.: Duke University Press, 2016.

Meriam Report on Indian Administration and the Survey of Conditions of the Indians in the US. https://www.gale.com/binaries/content/assets/gale-us-en/primary-sources/archives-unbound/primary-sources_archives-unbound_meriam-report-on-indian-administration-and-the-survey-of-conditions-of-the-indians-in-the-u.s.pdf.

Miller, Robert J. "The Doctrine of Discovery in American Indian Law." *Idaho Law Review* 42 (2005): 1.

Million, Dian. *Therapeutic Nations: Healing in an Age of Indigenous Human Rights*. Tucson: University of Arizona Press, 2013.

Million, Dian. "There Is a River in Me: Theory from Life." In *Theorizing Native Studies*, edited by Audra Simpson and Andrea Smith, 31–42. Durham, N.C.: Duke University Press, 2014.

MMIW. "MMIW USA." https://mmiwusa.org/.

Montoya v. United States, 180 U.S. 261, 266 (1900).

Morrison, Toni. *Playing in the Dark: Whiteness and the Literary Imagination*. Cambridge, Mass.: Harvard University Press, 1992.

Muñoz, José Esteban. *Disidentifications: Queers of Color and the Performance of Politics*. Minneapolis: University of Minnesota Press, 1999.

Newcomb, Steven T. *Pagans in the Promised Land: Decoding the Doctrine of Christian Discovery*. Golden, Colo.: Fulcrum, 2008.

Newton, Nell J. "Enforcing the Federal–Indian Trust Relationship after Mitchell." *Catholic University Law Review* 31 (1982): 635–84.

Owens, Louis. "As If an Indian Were Really an Indian: Native American Voices and Postcolonial Theory." In *Native American Representations: First Encounters, Distorted Images, and Literary Appropriations*, edited by Gretchen M. Bataille, 11–25. Lincoln: University of Nebraska Press, 2001.

Peltier, Leonard. *Prison Writings: My Life Is My Sun Dance*. New York: St. Martin's Press, 1999.

Piatote, Beth H. *Domestic Subjects: Gender, Citizenship, and Law in Native American Literature*. New Haven, Conn.: Yale University Press, 2013.

Piranesi in Rome. "Inscriptions: Colosseum." http://omeka.wellesley.edu/piranesi-rome/exhibits/show/colosseum/inscriptions#:~:text=Like%20many%20of%20the%20other.

Pratt, Richard H. *Battlefield and Classroom: Four Decades with the American Indian, 1867–1904*. Norman: University of Oklahoma Press, 2003.

Pratt, Richard H. *Official Report of the Nineteenth Annual Conference of Charities and Correction*, 46–59. 1892. Reprinted in Richard H. Pratt, "The Advantages of Mingling Indians with Whites," *Americanizing the American Indians: Writings by the "Friends of the Indian" 1880–1900* (Cambridge, Mass.: Harvard University Press, 1973), 260–71. http://historymatters.gmu.edu/d/4929.

Raheja, Michelle. "Visual Sovereignty." In *Native Studies Keywords*, edited by Stephanie Nohelani Teves, Michelle H. Raheja, and Andrea Smith, 25–34. Tucson: University of Arizona Press, 2015.

Roberts, Dorothy E. "Abolition Constitutionalism." *Harvard Law Review* 133 (2019): 3–122.

Roberts, Dorothy E. *Fatal Invention: How Science, Politics, and Big Business Re-create Race in the Twenty-First Century*. New York: New Press, 2012.

Robinson, Cedric J. *Black Marxism: The Making of the Black Radical Tradition*. Chapel Hill: University of North Carolina Press, 2000.

Robinson, Cedric J. *Black Movements in America*. New York: Routledge, 1997.

Robinson, Cedric J. *Forgeries of Memory and Meaning: Blacks and the Regimes of Race in American Theater and Film before World War II*. Chapel Hill: University of North Carolina Press, 2007.

Rodriguez, Dylan. *Forced Passages: Imprisoned Radical Intellectuals and the US Prison Regime*. Minneapolis: University of Minnesota Press, 2005.

Roy, Arundhati. *Public Power in the Age of Empire*. New York: Seven Stories Press, 2004.

Said, Edward W. *Culture and Imperialism*. New York: Knopf, 1993.

Savanna's Act. 25 U.S.C. § 5701 et seq. (2020).

Shanley, K. "The Indians America Loves to Love and Read: American Indian Identity and Cultural Appropriation." In *Native American Representations: First Encounters, Distorted Images, and Literary Appropriations*, edited by Gretchen M. Bataille, 26–51. Lincoln: University of Nebraska Press, 2001.

Silko, Leslie M. *Ceremony*. New York: Penguin, 1986.

Silman, Janet. *Enough Is Enough: Aboriginal Women Speak Out*. Toronto, Ont.: Women's Press, 1992.

Simpson, Audra. "Consent's Revenge." *Cultural Anthropology* 31, no. 3 (2016): 326–33. https://doi.org/10.14506/ca31.3.02.

Simpson, Audra. "On Ethnographic Refusal: Indigeneity, 'Voice' and Colonial Citizenship." *Junctures: Journal for Thematic Dialogue* 9 (December 2009): 67–80. https://junctures.org/index.php/junctures /article/view/66/60.

Simpson, Audra. "The Ruse of Consent and the Anatomy of 'Refusal': Cases from Indigenous North America and Australia." *Postcolonial Studies* 20, no. 1 (2017): 18–33. https://doi.org/10.1080/13688790.2017.1334283.

Simpson, Audra. "The State Is a Man: Theresa Spence, Loretta Saunders and the Gender of Settler Sovereignty." *Theory and Event* 19, no. 4 (2016). https://www.muse.jhu.edu/article/633280.

Simpson, Leanne B. *As We Have Always Done: Indigenous Freedom through Radical Resistance*. Minneapolis: University of Minnesota Press, 2017.

Sojoyner, Damien M. "Black Radicals Make for Bad Citizens: Undoing the Myth of the School to Prison Pipeline." *Berkeley Review of Education* 4, no. 2 (2013): 241–63. https://doi.org/10.5070/B84110021.

Sojoyner, Damien M. *First Strike: Educational Enclosures in Black Los Angeles*. Minneapolis: University of Minnesota Press, 2016.

Standing Bear, Luther. *My People the Sioux*. Boston: Houghton Mifflin, 1928.

Strong, Pauline T. *American Indians and the American Imaginary: Cultural Representation across the Centuries*. New York: Taylor and Francis, 2015.

TallBear, Kim. "An Indigenous, Feminist Approach to DNA Politics." In *Native American DNA: Tribal Belonging and the False Promise of Genetic Science*, 1–30. https://doi.org/10.5749/minnesota /9780816665853.003.0001.

Thomas, Deborah A. *Political Life in the Wake of the Plantation: Sovereignty, Witnessing, Repair*. Durham, N.C.: Duke University Press, 2019.

Trask, Haunani-Kay. *From a Native Daughter: Colonialism and Sovereignty in Hawai'i*. 2nd ed. Honolulu: University of Hawai'i Press, 1999.

United States v. Kagama. 118 U.S. 75 (1886).

Vaught, Sabina E. *Compulsory: Education and the Dispossession of Youth in a Prison School*. Minneapolis: University of Minnesota Press, 2017.

Vaught, Sabina E. "Vanishment: Girls, Punishment, and the Education State." *Teachers College Record* 121, no. 7 (2019): 1–36. https://doi .org/10.1177/016146811912100706.

Vizenor, Gerald. "Custer on the Slipstream." In *Walking the Clouds: An Anthology of Indigenous Science Fiction*, edited by Grace L. Dillon, 17–25. Tucson: University of Arizona Press, 2012.

Vizenor, Gerald. *Fugitive Poses: Native American Indian Scenes of Absence and Presence*. Lincoln: University of Nebraska Press, 1998.

Vizenor, Gerald. *Manifest Manners: Narratives on Postindian Survivance*. Lincoln: University of Nebraska Press, 1999.

Vizenor, Gerald. *The Trickster of Liberty: Native Heirs to a Wild Baronage*. Norman: University of Oklahoma Press, 2005.

Wadhwa, Anita. *Restorative Justice in Urban Schools: Disrupting the School-to-Prison Pipeline*. New York: Routledge, 2015.

Walker, Alan B. *Every Warrior Has His Own Song*. New York: iUniverse, 2010.

White, Louellyn. *Free to Be Mohawk: Indigenous Education at the Akwesasne Freedom School*. Norman: University of Oklahoma Press, 2015.

Wilkins, David E., and Tsianina Lomawaima. *Uneven Ground: American Indian Sovereignty and Federal Law*. Norman: University of Oklahoma, 2001.

Wilkins, David E., and Shelly Hulse Wilkins. *Dismembered: Native Disenrollment and the Battle for Human Rights*. Seattle: University of Washington Press, 2017.

Williams, Patricia J. *The Alchemy of Race and Rights: Diary of a Law Professor*. Cambridge, Mass.: Harvard University Press, 1991.

Williams, Patricia J. "On Being the Object of Property." *Signs: Journal of Women in Culture and Society* 14, no. 1 (1988). https://doi .org/10.1086/494489.

Williams, Rhiannon. "Prisoners Could Serve '1,000 Year Sentences in 8.5 Hours' in the Future." *The Telegraph*, March 18, 2014. https://www .businessinsider.com/prisoners-could-serve-1000-year-sentence-in -85-hours-in-the-future-2014-3.

Winder, Tanaya. *Why Storms Are Named After People and Bullets Remain Nameless*. CreateSpace Independent Publishing Platform, 2017.

Womack, Craig S. *Red on Red: Native American Literary Separatism*. Minneapolis: University of Minnesota Press, 1999.

Worcester v. Georgia, 31 U.S. 515 (1832).

Wynter, Sylvia. "On How We Mistook the Map for the Territory, and Re-imprisoned Ourselves in Our Unbearable Wrongness of Being, of *Désêtre*: Black Studies toward the Human Project." In *Not Only the Master's Tools: African-American Studies in Theory and Practice*, edited by Lewis R. Gordon and Jane Anna Gordon, 107–69. New York: Routledge, 2015.

Wynter, Sylvia. "Unsettling the Coloniality of Being/Power/Truth/ Freedom: Towards the Human, after Man, Its Overrepresentation—an Argument." *New Centennial Review* 3, no. 3 (2003): 257–337. https://doi .org/10.1353/ncr.2004.0015.

Zuberi, Tukufu. *Thicker than Blood (How Racial Statistics Lie)*. Minneapolis: University of Minnesota Press, 2003.

(Continued from page iii)

Forerunners: Ideas First

Ginger Nolan
The Neocolonialism of the Global Village

Joanna Zylinska
The End of Man: A Feminist Counterapocalypse

Robert Rosenberger
Callous Objects: Designs against the Homeless

William E. Connolly
Aspirational Fascism: The Struggle for Multifaceted Democracy under Trumpism

Chuck Rybak
UW Struggle: When a State Attacks Its University

Clare Birchall
Shareveillance: The Dangers of Openly Sharing and Covertly Collecting Data

la paperson
A Third University Is Possible

Kelly Oliver
Carceral Humanitarianism: Logics of Refugee Detention

P. David Marshall
The Celebrity Persona Pandemic

Davide Panagia
Ten Theses for an Aesthetics of Politics

David Golumbia
The Politics of Bitcoin: Software as Right-Wing Extremism

Sohail Daulatzai
Fifty Years of *The Battle of Algiers*: Past as Prologue

Gary Hall
The Uberfication of the University

Mark Jarzombek
Digital Stockholm Syndrome in the Post-Ontological Age

N. Adriana Knouf
How Noise Matters to Finance

Andrew Culp
Dark Deleuze

Akira Mizuta Lippit
Cinema without Reflection: Jacques Derrida's Echopoiesis and Narcissism Adrift

Sharon Sliwinski
Mandela's Dark Years: A Political Theory of Dreaming

Grant Farred
Martin Heidegger Saved My Life

Ian Bogost
The Geek's Chihuahua: Living with Apple

Shannon Mattern
Deep Mapping the Media City

Steven Shaviro
No Speed Limit: Three Essays on Accelerationism

Jussi Parikka
The Anthrobscene

Reinhold Martin
Mediators: Aesthetics, Politics, and the City

John Hartigan Jr.
Aesop's Anthropology: A Multispecies Approach

Bryan McKinley Jones Brayboy (Lumbee) is President's Professor, senior adviser to the president, and vice president of social advancement at Arizona State University and the coeditor of the *Journal of American Indian Education*.

Jeremiah Chin is assistant professor of law at St. Thomas University College of Law.

Sabina Vaught is professor of education at the University of Pittsburgh and the author of *Compulsory: Education and the Dispossession of Youth in a Prison School* (Minnesota, 2017).